WHAT FUTURE FOR EDUCATION?

What Future for Education?

Brian Simon

LAWRENCE & WISHART
LONDON

Lawrence & Wishart Limited
144a Old South Lambeth Road
London SW8 1XX

First published 1992
Copyright © Brian Simon, 1992

Photoset in North Wales by
Derek Doyle & Associates, Mold, Clwyd
Printed and bound in Great Britain by
Billing & Sons of Worcester

Contents

Introduction and Acknowledgements

Education has passed through four traumatic years, following the publication of the Consultation Papers presaging the 'Great Education Reform Bill' in the summer of 1987. These were themselves preceded by some ten years of unceasing criticism from politicians, industrialists and the media who combined to establish education as the scapegoat for Britain's poor relative performance in terms of economic and industrial development. So the scenario was constructed for an attempt at a radical revision of procedures, largely promulgated by the many Tory right-wing groupings which established a certain intellectual hegemony and had also gained the ear of the then leader of the Conservative Party (Margaret Thatcher). The outcome was the Education Act of 1988.

But all has not been plain sailing, even for the government, whose massive parliamentary majority over these years underlay legislative measures. Opting out, city technology colleges, open enrolment, testing – all these and many other aspects of the new policy never succeeded in gaining popular support. Indeed, toward the end of the period public opinion polls showed massive concern with the way things were going. Partly as a result, the pace of change was now accelerated; there is no sign, however, that the new measures are any more widely acceptable.

One feature of this whole development has been the deliberate attempt substantially to reduce the powers of local government, and especially to break its close concern with the provision of education under local control. The attempt to swing the whole system to determination by market forces – to establish a market in education – has fuelled the move to deprive local authorities of their historic role as providers and planners, having the interests of local populations at heart, present and future. This has led many to feel that the whole edifice is at risk; that the objective of providing equally for all, which necessarily motivated local systems, was being overturned by the substitution of conditions which set each against all in the struggle to survive and prosper at the expense of others. Confrontation and conflict was taking the place of co-operation, solidarity and mutual assistance. What, then, is the future for education?

It is clear that big issues are at stake; issues which will have to be resolved in the near future. As this book goes to press, in the early autumn of 1991, a general election is in the air and electoral fever is mounting. Whoever is victorious will inherit a real legacy of strife, confrontation, widespread demoralisation. To cope with these and restore a generally agreed sense of direction will be the task of the new government. Positive outcomes are essential for the health of the country.

This book comprises articles and lectures written or delivered over the last four years, and presented in chronological order, together with a final extended chapter written in the summer of 1991. All, without exception, are directly concerned with the nature and impact of the Education Act of 1988. Each analyses different aspects of these developments, though there are, of course, ongoing common features. All are reprinted as originally published, with only very minor emendations where necessary, particularly to avoid repetition.

I have many acknowledgements to make. To *Marxism Today* for permitting the reproduction of 'Lessons in Elitism', written in some haste immediately after the publication of the Consultation Papers at the end of July 1987 (and before the publication of the Bill itself), and published in September 1987. This presented my immediate reactions to the measures proposed, all of which were in fact included in the Bill and Act. This critique was followed up in March 1988 with the publication of *Bending the Rules, the Baker 'Reform' of Education*, a critical analysis of the Bill, its origins and probable outcomes, which went through three editions (and four printings) during the year.

I must thank also the British Education Management and Administration Society for inviting me to lecture to its annual conference in September 1988 (one month after the Act received Royal Assent) on 'Maintaining Progress towards a Fully Comprehensive System' – an evaluation of the prospects for comprehensive education under the new dispensation, which forms Chapter 2 of this volume. The educational journal *Forum*, of which I have been co-editor for many years (but no longer), kindly gave permission to reprint 'Thatcher's Third Tier, or Bribery and Corruption', which contains an analysis of developments in relation to opting out (grant maintained schools) and city technology colleges over approximately two years following the passage of the Act (Chapter 3). This was published in Vol.32, No.3 (Summer 1990).

My thanks are also due to the Lawrence Stenhouse Memorial Trust, which arranges an annual lecture at the conference of the British Education Research Association in memory of that most innovative of educators, for permitting reproduction of 'The National Curriculum, School Organisation and the Teacher' (Chapter 4), originally published by the Lawrence Stenhouse Memorial Trust. This was delivered in August 1990 – just two years after the Education Act 1988 received Royal Assent. It focuses on the relevance of Lawrence Stenhouse's thinking to developments in the contemporary scene. 'What Future for Education?' (Chapter 5), which tackles the issue of the market in education, is the centenary lecture delivered at the School of Education, University of Newcastle-upon-Tyne, and I am grateful to Professor Tony Edwards and the School for permission to include it in this collection. This was originally published as 'The Future of Education: Which Way?' by the School of Education, University of Newcastle-upon-Tyne. It focuses on contrasting values driving the educational system.

Finally I have also to thank Professor Patricia Broadfoot and the British Education Research Association for permission to include a paper I was asked to contribute to a seminar organised by the BERA Task Group on Assessment in July, 1991. Here I was invited to give my own policy assessment as to the causes lying behind the 1988 Education Act (Chapter 6). The final chapter, as already mentioned, was written specifically for this volume during the summer of 1991, and attempts to define exactly where the world of education now finds itself – no easy task, incidentally.

I owe a special debt of gratitude to Professor David Ashton for discussions on the relation between education and changes in the youth labour market referred to in Chapter 6, as also to Kevin Fitzgerald and Gwen Wallace for their assistance in helping me to grasp the real significance of the local management of schools initiative discussed in Chapter 7. To Stephen Hayward of Lawrence and Wishart also my thanks for encouraging the publication of this volume, and for continuous and thoughtful editorial assistance.

I hope this book may do something to help alert people to the full seriousness of our present predicament; and perhaps strengthen the growing determination to find a more fruitful road to the future than that provided for us over the last four years.

Brian Simon
25 September 1991

Abbreviations

ACE	Advisory Centre for Education
AMMA	Assistant Masters and Mistresses Association
ASB	Aggregated Schools Budget
BERA	British Education Research Association
CAC	Central Advisory Council
CARE	Centre for Applied Research in Education
CASE	Campaign for the Advancement of State Education
CEO	Chief Education Officer
CLEA	Conference of Local Education Authorities
CSE	Certificate of Secondary Education
CTC	City Technology College
DES	Department of Education and Science
ERA	Education Reform Act
GCE	General Certificate of Education
GCSE	General Certificate of Secondary Education
GDP	Gross Domestic Product
GMS	Grant Maintained School
HMI	Her Majesty's Inspector
ILEA	Inner London Education Authority
LEA	Local Education Authority
LMS	Local Management of Schools
NCPTA	National Confederation of Parent Teacher Associations

NCC	National Curriculum Council
NUS	National Union of Students
NUT	National Union of Teachers
PAT	Professional Association of Teachers
PSB	Potential Schools Budget
SAT	Standard Assessment Task
SEAC	Schools Examination and Assessment Council
SEO	Society of Education Officers
TGAT	Task Group for Assessment and Testing

1 Lessons in Elitism*

Having brought almost the entire educational system to its knees, through the adoption of strict monetarist policies under the reign of Keith Joseph, the Tory Party is now set on gaining electoral advantage through a basic restructuring and 'reform' of the whole system. Such, at least, seems the main motivation for a measure that is to take a large chunk of parliamentary time from the start of the October session through to the summer. We are in for a period of sharply-fought educational politics.

'We are going much further with education than we ever thought of doing before,' Margaret Thatcher told her favourite journalist, Sir David English, in an extended interview early in May. 'You mean there's going to be a revolution in the running of schools if you're re-elected?' asked her interviewer. 'That's right,' she answered. 'Money would flow to good schools and good headmasters (sic).'[1] 'Tories: We'll End School Tyranny', headlined the *Mail* in huge black letters. 'The return of a Conservative government today will mean the break-up of the state education system which has existed since 1944,' wrote Peter Wilby, education correspondent of the *Independent*, on election day. He advised his readers not to vote Tory if they wished to save the system from destruction.

* First published in September 1987.

Thatcher confirmed, after the election, that the proposed education reform had a directly political purpose. 'Just as we gained political support in the last election from people who had acquired their own homes and shares,' she claimed, 'so we shall secure still further our political base in 1991-92 – by giving people a real say in education and housing.' The proposed Bill is 'the key to the future: the biggest and most important legislation of the forthcoming parliamentary session'.[2]

The pressure is on to push the Bill through at maximum speed. Protests – by Jack Straw, the new shadow education spokesman, Sheffield city's education committee, and many others – that the time allowed for consultation was ludicrously short, and badly timed, have been met by Education Secretary Kenneth Baker's appeal to the exigencies of the parliamentary timetable (determined, of course, by the government). During July, several 'consultation' papers were issued, the most important dealing with financial delegation, open enrolment, 'opting out' and, above all, with the proposed national curriculum. Officials at the Department of Education and Science have clearly been working under pressure – even if the outlines of the Bill were evidently drawn up before the election. On 3 July the DES announced that consultation papers 'can be expected in days rather than weeks ... to allow a consultation period of at least three months'.[3] In fact, the most recent of these, on the curriculum – 40 pages of closely spaced type on A4 paper – was only published on 24 July, allowing a consultation period on this most controversial of issues of only just over two months, till the end of September. The Education Act of 1944, with which the 'Baker Bill' is being compared, was preceded by at least two years of consultation, and this during a war. Associations of all kinds, groups and individuals prepared their submissions and, in many cases, published them for open discussion well before the bill was finally drawn up. The same is true of the 1918 Fisher Act. The procedures used in the present case make it abundantly clear that there is no intention whatever to engage in serious consultation. The government knows what it wants, and is going to impose it by *force majeure* relying on its 100-plus majority in the Commons.

What is the overall Tory strategy? Its main thrust is clear enough, and indeed has been overtly stated by Baker. Fundamentally, the objective is, through downgrading and by-passing local authorities, to establish a whole mini-'system' of quasi-independent schools between the prestigious 'public' schools on the one hand, and local systems of primary and secondary schools on the other. These would serve the 'yuppie' (and other) strata between the working class and the really wealthy. 'I want a much greater degree of variety and independence in the running of schools,' Baker told Stuart Maclure, the editor of the *Times Educational Supplement*.[4] 'I want to see a greater amount of variety and choice.'[5]

By appealing to 'variety' and 'choice', Baker is utilising an old-established Tory ploy. In the past, this argument was used to legitimise the tripartite system, as well as to give support for voluntary (church) schools when these were under attack. Today it is used to legitimise a variety of types or levels of schools, subsidised from public funds in various, often hidden, ways (e.g. through the assisted places scheme), sometimes charging fees, and designed for intermediate social strata − professional, business and technocratic. While the

Tories want a *variety* of schools, however, they are also arguing for *uniformity* in the curriculum where, they now claim, there is too much 'variety'.

Not everyone, even on the Tory side, agrees with this 'historic reform' as Baker describes it. To compare the proposed Bill with what Rab Butler did, said Edward Heath in the debate on the Queen's speech, 'would make the great man turn in his grave'. The various propositions being discussed (opting out, charging fees, etc.) were

> part of the supermarket mentality in many right-wing quarters which believed education could be packaged like food. I warn the Chancellor and the Secretary of State many of us feel passionately about these matters, and we will not stand idly by and let them happen.[6]

(Heath, it is worth remembering, agreed in 1968-69 on the need to abolish the 11-plus and extend comprehensive schooling.)

In March a group of 'moderate' Tories formed the Conservative Education Association to support the state sector and counter the hard Right within the party, while, as we shall see, Tory-controlled local authorities are also on the move. All may not be plain sailing after all.

As for the bill itself, it is evident that both strategy and tactics have been carefully worked out, largely by various right-wing groups and 'think-tanks' which have been very active in the last few years.[7] Vouchers are not, apparently, to be brought in, in spite of much pressure. Instead, a more subtle set of linked measures are to be relied on to have the desired effect – that is, to push the whole system toward a degree, at least, of privatisation, establishing a base which could be further exploited

later. Considered separately, there may be something to be said for some of these measures (for
instance, financial delegation to heads and governors); but considered as a set of interrelated
measures, as they must be, each can be seen to
provide its specific thrust towards the desired
objectives.

There is, first, the proposal to devolve financial
responsibility for running schools more or less
completely to the heads and governors. Some
experience, though limited in scope, has already
been gained in Cambridgeshire and elsewhere.
There are a large number of problems here, such as
over-burdening untrained heads with financial
management (was it proposed, asked Heath, to
recruit 31,500 bursars?), but of course the main
objective is to loosen the schools from the hands of
the local authorities, and encourage them to take
the first step towards more advanced forms of
independence.

Second, there is the proposal to allow 'open
enrolment' (within a very broad limit) to all schools.
Local authorities, in order to plan the contraction of
their systems (due to falling rolls) rationally, with
the aim of maximising the educational effectiveness
of the system as a whole, have had powers till now to
fix a limit to each school's intake. It is this which is
to go. Schools, it is argued, must have the right to
admit as many pupils as parents wish to send them,
and so be permitted to expand considerably (and
suddenly). Unpopular schools, conversely, must go
to the wall – and be closed as a result of the
operation of this form of market forces. The full
implications of this proposal will be discussed
shortly. In terms of overall strategy, however, the
meaning of this step is clear. Popular schools, now

with more or less full financial responsibility, will soon begin to differentiate themselves from the others. This provides the springboard for the next step – opting out – also to be provided for in the Bill.

Third, it seems likely that the Bill will include clauses legitimising the charging of fees by schools for certain activities.[8] This was, of course, the issue where Thatcher put her foot in it during the election campaign, when she said that the objective was to charge fees in publicly maintained schools, only to be corrected by Baker. But fees for 'extras' seems a different thing – if, in fact, it is basically similar. The 1944 Act says that 'no fees shall be charged in respect of the education provision in any maintained school'. The intention appears to be to reverse this clause, and to permit such fees for 'extras' (which of course today include essential equipment and materials) to be charged. In some local authority areas this is already permitted, but to legalise the process through a new statute is a different matter. Clearly this fits in to the general strategy very precisely. Popular schools in affluent areas will be permitted to charge such fees, as will others of course; but this will provide such schools with the opportunity further to differentiate themselves from the ordinary run of schools, and to some extent to narrow their clientele to the more affluent section of the local population. So now the school is poised for break-out.

This takes us directly to the most important of the probable new clauses – that concerned with 'opting out', on which a 'consultation' paper has been issued. The proposal is that schools that wish to (as indicated by a simple majority vote of parents) may apply to 'opt out' from the local system of which they are a part, and become 'grant maintained' schools, receiving a grant directly from the DES instead of the local authority. All formal relations with the local authority would by this means be broken. The school would become 'semi-independent', receiving the bulk of its finance directly from the state. A further direct effect would be that the local system, as a 'system', would also be broken. Once again the full implications of this will be discussed below. Here the main emphasis is on the thrust of policy – and on the interrelations between the various measures being proposed.

The final step in this carefully designed progression – though I should make it clear that this goes beyond anything proposed in the Bill, and is denied by those behind this measure – would be a bid for 'independence' by successful opted-out ('grant-maintained') schools; that is, their recruitment to the independent sector. This could be achieved through a combination of fee-paying by parents (who will anyway be increasingly paying for 'extras'), and support from the Exchequer through a large extension of the assisted places schemes, by which fees of individual pupils are paid directly by the DES. Many independent schools already rely on this source of funds for their very existence – it seems probable that several were saved from bankruptcy when the measure was introduced in the early 1980s. There has already been talk of just such an extension of the assisted places scheme. By this means, the objective of increasing the provision of purely 'independent' schools for sections of the middle strata becomes a practical possibility.

Nothing has been said about the twenty-plus city technology colleges which the government now proposes to establish, relying partially on funds extracted (reluctantly) from industry. But it should be remembered that, through this means also, the 'variety' of semi-independent schools Baker favours will be enhanced over the next few years (again at the expense of disrupting local systems).[9]

There is space here only very briefly to report the reactions of responsible educationalists to some of these proposals. The open enrolment and opting out clauses are clearly identified by all as comprising the central thrust of this section of the Bill. They will have the combined and clearly desired effect of acting both as stages for the enhancement of the semi-independent sector, and of depressing and downgrading the mass of ordinary schools for ordinary people's children, which will remain – at the bottom of the pile – under local authority control. They will also make it extremely difficut, if not impossible, for local authorities to plan tertiary (sixteen to nineteen) reorganisation, or any other restructuring of their systems, necessitated as a result of falling rolls or other demographic changes. And so they will add to the general loss of morale and downgrading of the mass of schools for working people.

All this has been very clearly seen by those most intimate with local administration. The whole scheme has been condemned by Sir Roy Harding, general secretary of the Society of Education Officers (and a distinguished ex-Chief Education Officer himself). In an article entitled 'Careering off down the wrong road', Harding strongly condemned the proposals, which he describes as a U-turn 'from the encouragement of good planning to its negation'; if these measures are implemented, he argued, standards in the schools would be bound to fall 'and it is likely there will be a fall for most children'. The effect of a school opting out from the local system

will be to disrupt it. Such proposals, Harding
suggested, must be amended by another U-turn; the
government must 'show renewed concern for
improved standards by introducing legislation
which allows LEAs to plan school and staff provision
so that all pupils can have a broad, balanced,
relevant and appropriately differentiated curriculum'.[10] This is a reference to exhortations in the
government's 1985 White Paper, *Better Schools*.

Another to point out the implications of opting out
is Tessa Blackstone, ex-professor of educational
administration, formerly Deputy Education Officer
at the Inner London Education Authority and now
master of Birkbeck College, London University.
'Children's futures', she concluded, 'are now threatened by a scheme casually destructive of the best in
the maintained system, dangerously divisive, and
administratively unworkable.'[11] Even the *Times
Educational Supplement* is contemptuous.[12] The
proposal as it stands 'is going to raise costs and
lower efficiency'. Open enrolment itself means 'the
negation of planning'. If market forces are to prevail,
'Planning will, in future, be retrospective; a matter
of picking up the bits and presiding over the
bankruptcies after the consumers have made their
educational purchases.' It is extremely doubtful, if
these measures are implemented, whether 'it makes
any sense ... to talk about a "system" at the local
level'. A 'blight' will be put 'on all plans for
restructuring, closures and mergers'.[13]

It must surely be clear that professional opinion is
totally opposed both to the open enrolment proposal
and that concerning opting out. It is on these
grounds that many argue that the government's
so-called 'Great Education Reform Bill' in practice
means the actual break-up of the state education

system as we have known it. In the circumstances, these measures are beginning to appear totally irresponsible, as also do (if to a lesser degree) the government's proposed clauses concerning the Inner London Education Authority (ILEA) – perhaps the largest and most experienced education authority in the world. Here, the government is pursuing what the *Times Higher Education Supplement* describes as a 'sordid vendetta'. Baker is determined to break up the ILEA 'against all sense and against the wishes of the overwhelming majority of the parents'. So here 'anything goes'.[14] The proposal is that local boroughs may have the right again to 'opt out' from the ILEA and go it alone. Wandsworth, Westminster, Kensington and Chelsea, all well-heeled Tory authorities, are planning to do just that; but in this case, developments are likely to prove politically embarrassing to the government. A full analysis of the implications of these proposals concludes that 'One sure factor is that it will cost the government a lot of money to break up the ILEA,' and that the measures proposed will turn schools into 'a major focus of political activity'.[15]

So much for what might be called the structural aspects of the 'revolution' promised by Thatcher. But there is another aspect to this Bill. As mentioned earlier, while the Tories feel there has been too little variety among types of school, they also feel there has been too much in what is taught in them. A centrally imposed clamp-down is now to take place. From now on all English and Welsh children must learn the same things, as more or less precisely defined within a 'national curriculum'. Furthermore, all children must be subjected to a series of precisely defined tests – to provide 'bench-marks', as Baker puts it – at the age of seven, eleven, fourteen and sixteen. All this is to be statutorily determined through legislation. The wheel has come full circle.

Baker is on firmer ground, in terms of the time allowed for 'consultation', when he argues that there has been much discussion of the curriculum; what he does not mention, however, is that much of it has been severely critical of the increasingly energetic and ruthless thrust towards central control in this area, from both local authorities and teachers. A Mori poll showed recently that 65 per cent of teachers believe that the Secretary of State has sought too much power in running schools.[16] It is, however, fair to say that there probably is a broad consensus that a common core of subjects (or activities) is desirable – even a common curriculum. Those pioneering the move to comprehensive education back in the 1950s and early 1960s (including this author) certainly believed that here was an opportunity to offer *all* pupils access to knowledge, science and culture, and that to differentiate the curriculum for different groups of children was both arbitrary and divisive.

But those so arguing, then and now, hold that, if generally accepted 'guidelines' covering the curriculum are to be offered, these must be determined as a result of full and democratic discussion by all those involved, particularly the teachers. And that there needs to be some forum established for discussion of such matters where plans and proposals can be evolved. The idea that a precisely defined curriculum, covering the ages five to sixteen should be defined largely by civil servants at the DES (who are not educationalists, and have not themselves had any experience of actually teaching children), is and always has been entirely unacceptable.[17] The result is likely to be a massive alienation of the teaching force of the country who, if this proposal is actually implemented, will find themselves increasingly de-skilled and further down-graded – as the correspondence columns of the national newspapers are already showing.

The curriculum consultation paper, for which a mere two months at the height of the summer is allowed for response, is a typical product of a remote, managerially-inclined bureaucracy. It is based on the concept that the curriculum is something to be 'delivered' to the child – as if it were a package of fish and chips – and that the extent to which he or she absorbs it can be precisely measured at specific ages by a series of tests. Education is about the development of human abilities and skills, as well as the 'absorption' of knowledge. But this is entirely left out of the account. That said, the actual content of the package is unimaginatively academic. The curriculum is defined in terms of subjects, as it originally was (when the state last intervened here) back in 1904. This 'state curriculum', it is proposed, is to take up between 80 and 90 per cent of the pupil's time, leaving only some 15 per cent for any kind of option or special interest. All, it seems, are to do the same curriculum, in whatever type of school – except that the government's own specially cherished new schools (the city technology colleges) are to be exempt, as are (unsurprisingly) the 'independent' schools. This a curriculum for the masses. Its purpose is control.

Although a bow is made in the direction of teacher initiative, if this curriculum is imposed, the scope for imaginative teaching, for instance for the integration of subjects in line with the development of modern knowledge, for independent initiative by individual schools, groups of schools, or local systems, will be tightly constricted. Sheffield, for instance, is now involved in a highly imaginative and successful curriculum reform project covering all their schools, both primary and secondary, with the aim of developing new curricula and procedures in line with modern developments in knowledge and in pedagogy. Unless a special dispensation is to be granted, all such creative work and thinking will go for nothing. The whole teacher-based curriculum reform movement, which is widespread and extremely positive, is at risk. No wonder Harry Rée, a distinguished ex-head and professor, has protested. At a stroke, he wrote to the *Independent*, all we have been working for all our lives is being wiped out.[18]

The curriculum paper lays down generally how much time should be spent on each subject at each stage, though focusing especially on the last two years (fourteen to sixteen). It also lays down when the 'bench-mark' testing is to take place, and how these test results are to be communicated to parliament, the public generally, employers, the local community, parents, teachers and even the children. The focus on the value and accuracy of such tests as are available (or will be developed) is naïve, to say the least (here the bureaucratic character of the paper stands out most vividly). This is an exceptionally difficult area, as all educationalists know very well, but the DES officials responsible for the paper simply sweep such problems aside. Tests of this kind, writes Roger Murphy, head of the examinations and assessment unit at Southampton University, will almost certainly become 'crude remote measures of a very limited part of the achievement of primary pupils'. Instead, he argues, teachers should be given the training and resources needed 'to develop their own role in assessment of all children throughout the primary years' and not only at seven and eleven.[19] The bench-mark proposals are probably the worst aspect of a policy which, overall, is likely to severely damage the schools and their pupils.

As for the national curriculum, Denis Lawton, a curriculum expert and director of London University's Institute of Education, and Clyde Chitty write that 'a national standardisation curriculum and external tests to assess achievement may well recreate the situation in late Victorian England when the vast majority of children were educated only to pass exams' (a reference to the 'payment by results' system). The proposal 'confuses education with training', the former being far more complex and difficult to evaluate. 'Education is about enriching a student's view of the world: not training him or her to give trite answers to complex questions.' We need, Lawton and Chitty write, 'to free the proposal for a national curriculum from the accompanying notion of age-related bench-mark testing which will simply act as a straitjacket on the entire system'. Above all, they conclude,

> We need to convince the government that their plans will acquire no credibility with educationalists and teachers while a national curriculum continues to be viewed by politicians and civil servants as a convenient bureaucratic device for exercising control over what goes on in schools.[20]

This they see as the main objective of the whole exercise. There are many who will agree with them.

The 'Great Education Reform Bill', it seems, comprises a very real threat to the viability of the country's education system as a whole, and also to the system of local government in which it has traditionally found its base. Whether it involves the actual break-up of the system as we have known it, as Peter Wilby has suggested, remains to be seen. This must partly depend on how effective a resistance to government plans can be mounted during the coming months. There is certainly scope and backing for such a resistance – to a scheme, or set of schemes, which can appear almost adventurous, but whose outcome, even if fully implemented in their pure form, must be highly problematic.

Where are the forces that could mount such an effective resistance? Those most directly concerned are the local authorities, whose systems are threatened; teachers, whose autonomy and procedures in their profession are at risk; and parents, whose children attending normal local authority schools would certainly suffer – that is, the great bulk of parents. These forces, clearly *potentially* powerful if they can work together, form the centres from which resistance can be mounted. Since the Bill is to be introduced in parliament in October or November, and is to go through the normal parliamentary processes of debate and discussion (probably shortened by much use of the guillotine) in the winter, spring and perhaps early summer of next year, opposition, to be effective, must partly take the form of amendments either nullifying the proposed clauses, or radically modifying them in the direction of more democratic (and sensible) alternatives. Opposition, therefore, must be focused on parliament (both Houses, since it is expected that the House of Lords may have a large part to play due to pressure of parliamentary business), where it will be led by Labour's new shadow spokesman on education, Jack Straw (likely to be capable of a far more effective opposition than his predecessor). But resistance to the government's intentions cannot, of course, be left to parliament alone. A broad movement needs to be developed outside as the main means of ensuring that the real significance of these proposals are widely grasped among the population as a whole – in face of what is likely to be a continuing barrage of Tory propaganda in favour of the proposals, seen as central to building new bases of electoral support for 1991-92.

Already the constituent members of these oppositional groupings have begun to make their positions clear. In July the Council of Local Education Authorities (CLEA), which includes Conservative authorities as well as Labour, Alliance and 'hung' councils, decided to establish a standing conference on education to argue its case favouring local control, and presumably to conduct a fight for it. The fact that Tory councils supported this initiative reflects again divisions within the Tory Party on this whole issue.

As far as the teachers are concerned, almost unanimous opposition to Baker's proposals can be expected; but how effective can this be made? Quick off the mark has been the National Union of Teachers, which has a strong resolution on a number of issues (condemning the national curriculum and testing) for the TUC this month. The NUT has already officially protested about the opting out proposals ('we believe grant-maintained schools will be elitist in character and divisive in their effect'), and about the bench-mark testing proposals ('it is an educational nonsense to force children through rigid tests so early and so often'). Of course the teachers have other battles with the government under way, particularly those relating to the loss of negotiating rights, and these will also be strongly pressed. But it is to be hoped that the unions generally will get their act together in opposing, or proposing positive alternatives, to the main clauses of the Bill which threaten the maintained system as a whole. United actions will be the more effective the earlier they get off the ground.

Finally, the main parents' association, the National Confederation of Parent-Teacher Associations, to take one example, is in no sense the government's poodle. Uniting 6,400 parent-teacher associations across the country, with 40 local executive committees, it can claim the leading role among such organisations (there are others; for instance, the Campaign for the Advancement of State Education). Indignant at the time allowed for 'consultation' (and its timing), the NCPTA has officially protested to Baker personally that the 'consultation' period should have been timed to coincide with the summer holidays when children are at home. Having taken a highly progressive line on a number of educational issues recently, there is little doubt that the confederation, and other organisations, will express clear and positive views in defence of the public system of education.

Government ministers are said (by an experienced observer) to have been 'startled by the passionate support for the state education and health services' voiced during the election; if the united voices of 'parents, churches, teachers and the local authorities can be mobilised in opposition to the Education bill', writes Maureen O'Connor, positive results may be achieved.[21] I believe this to be a correct assessment. The next few months will provide the test.

Notes and References

1. *Daily Mail*, 1 May 1987.
2. *Independent*, 17 July 1987.
3. *Times Educational Supplement*, 3 July 1987.
4. Ibid., 3 March 1987.
5. Baker explained that about 7 per cent or so go to independent schools and 93 per cent to the state maintained sector. 'I'm responsible for that. What I think is striking in the British educational system is that there is nothing in between. Now the city technology colleges are a half-way house. I would like to see many more half-way houses, a greater choice, a greater variety. I think many parents would as well.' *Times Educational Supplement*, 3 April 1987.
6. *Times Educational Supplement*, 10 July 1987.
7. For a useful assessment of these, see Peter Wilby and Simon Midgley, *Independent*, 23 July 1987.
8. A consultation document was issued on this after this article was published (in October 1987). The outcome was that school governing bodies and LEAs must have a 'charging policy' (Section 110). Sections 106-111 of the Education Act redefine 'free education' and clarify the powers and duties of local education authorities with regard to charges for services. Stuart Maclure, *Education Re-formed*, 1988. [This note added in September 1991.]
9. For a useful (critical) evaluation of this initiative, see Clyde Chitty, 'The Commodification of Education', *Forum*, Summer 1987.
10. *Times Educational Supplement*, 3 July 1987.
11. *Guardian*, 9 June 1987.
12. *Times Educational Supplement*, 17 July 1987.
13. It seems that Baker has already imposed his own 'blight' on local authority reorganisation plans. It was reported early in August that no fewer than 90 such plans are awaiting approval by the Secretary of State, and that 'Some have been before Mr Baker for as long as eighteen months.' *Guardian*, 3 August 1987.
14. *Times Higher Education Supplement*, 31 July 1987.
15. Julia Hagedorn, 10 July 1987. [The ILEA was, of course, finally abolished outright by the 1988 Education Act – B.S. September 1991.]
16. *Times Educational Supplement*, 12 June 1987.
17. The consultation paper on the curriculum and assessment (the 'Red Book') in fact announced the appointment of subject working groups and the Task Group on Assessment and Testing (TGAT), having the functions of proposing programmes of study and procedures for assessment and testing respectively. The importance of these proposals was overlooked in this article. [This note added September 1991.]
18. Harry Judge, ex-comprehensive head and later director of the Department of Educational Studies at Oxford University, has also protested. Teachers in future would be 'shackled to a national curriculum in the worst traditions of centralised countries', he told

the CLEA conference. Baker's legislation would turn teachers into 'an oppressed bureaucracy'. *TES*, 17 July 1987.
19. *Forum*, Autumn 1987.
20. *Ibid.*
21. *Guardian*, 23 June 1987.

2 Maintaining Progress Towards a Fully Comprehensive System*

This title, which was given me, begs some questions, and raises some more. What do we mean by a 'fully comprehensive system'? However we define it, has there in fact been progress towards it? Is this progress of such a character that it can be 'maintained' – is there some inner, or for that matter external, dynamic that can take it forward, in spite of the new initiatives by the government embodied in the new 'Reform' Act? How will these new initiatives affect what might be called 'the comprehensiveness' of comprehensive education?

Clearly, in some respects, it's a cold climate now for comprehensive education. In a recent speech a responsible government spokesman – after stating (or this is how he was reported) that 'awareness of capitalist values should be the starting point for the national curriculum', and that 'to have an elementary grasp of capitalism and the enterprise culture is a moral virtue', apparently concluded by saying that, in the future, 'we will be evolving our educational system into more and more specialised, differentiated schools'.[1] This gentleman was, until recently, minister having responsibility for schools,

* Delivered as a paper in September 1988.

34

so his utterances should be taken seriously. He did not, apparently, envisage future progress as being towards a fully comprehensive system. What he seems to be suggesting – a system of specialised, differentiated schools – is the precise opposite. How far are his views widespread among the powers that be?

I am not going to make the case for comprehensive schooling. A lot might also be said, and perhaps needs to be said, about inner organisation and structure, about ethos and procedures, perhaps about relationships between schools in comprehensive systems, and above all about the curriculum. But that the basic system for pupils aged from five to sixteen, and perhaps to eighteen, should be comprehensive – that is, non-selective – I propose to take for granted. The case has been argued, in differing contexts, for the last 30 or 40 years, and indeed more, though admittedly not all are yet convinced. More important, in a practical sense, perhaps, is that local populations have consistently and *insistently* opted for such systems at crucial moments – and, significantly, *most* insistently when such systems have been under threat. The repeal of the 1976 Act in 1979 did not halt the swing towards comprehensive education; important (if peripheral) areas like Cumbria and Cornwall only then decided finally to go comprehensive – in the former case with very widespread public support. The attempt to turn the clock back in Solihull and elsewhere in the winter of 1983-84 totally failed, due to the profound, indignant and highly organised reactions of local populations and teachers (but mainly the former). Even over the last nine years, a key indicator – the number of grammar schools within maintained systems – has shown a steady decline from over 300 to 1979 to about 150 in 1988. These latter have found it necessary to band themselves together in an embattled system of self-defence, recently, incidentally, addressed and encouraged by the Secretary of State himself. The areas of the country where selective systems still function – Canute-like outposts of an unregretted past – have progressively narrowed. It is surely very clear that the answer to the question: has there been consistent progress towards comprehensive education – or to comprehensive systems? must be *yes*. Nor, in terms of local authority maintained systems does it show any sign of being halted. I think I am right in saying that not a single authority has ever moved deliberately from a comprehensive to a selective system. And there have been very many which have changed their political complexion at various times over the years – sometimes at quite crucial moments. Manchester and the ILEA are cases in point – but there have been many more.

My conclusion is that, in spite of all the criticism, even abuse, that has been thrown at the schools over the last fifteen years or so; and in spite of definite weaknesses within the schools themselves particularly in certain specific areas of the country, which external circumstances have made it difficult to overcome, the comprehensive system is here to stay. The social, economic and, if you like, scientific and technological changes that lie behind the movement – in the sense of enhanced aspirations and the demand for a longer and more rewarding school life – have shown immense power, when transformed specifically into the pattern of schooling desired by the mass of the people in this country. At this stage, as the late twentieth century gradually merges into the twenty-first, proposals to return to selection and

early differentiation fail to address the real issues –
to match the requirements of contemporary circumstances. It is not only that, as we know only too well,
such a pattern necessarily involves injustice to
many – those rejected from the more prestigious
differentiated schools. More important, all now
surely agree that we are living in an age when *every
child* needs access to an all-round, humanist
education embracing science and technology; that
this is essential if we are to face up to the challenge
both of the present and the future. Isn't this what
the so-called 'National Curriculum' is all about? By
what process of reasoning is it possible to argue both
for a *uniform curriculum*, and systems of *differentiated, specialised schools*?

So perhaps we can establish, as our starting point,
that there has been and still is progress towards a
comprehensive system. With a good deal of trauma
and a colossal amount of effort, which should not go
unhonoured and unsung, we have made and are still
making this transition. The DES itself acknow-
ledged this at the start of the notorious Yellow Book
passed to the Prime Minister's advisers in the
summer of 1976 – the briefing for Callaghan's
Ruskin speech. We have just brought about, they
said there, 'the greatest reorganisation of secondary
schooling in our educational history'. This has been
'a magnificent job', done in the attempt to provide 'a
genuinely universal free (system of) secondary
education'.[2] Critics, of course, and they certainly
have a point, say that the DES has consistently
tended to exaggerate the extent and character of the
movement, at least when a sympathetic government
was in power, claiming as 'comprehensive' many
schools that, due to creaming, are not genuinely so.
And of course our comprehensive system, or set of

systems, is in fact riven with competitive forms in various ways and to a different extent in different parts of the country. Scotland and Wales are certainly both further advanced in the direction of achieving *fully* comprehensive systems than we are in England. What we need to do, I suggest, is to search out these weaknesses, overcome them, and so achieve a more fully or more genuinely comprehensive system here in England also. That, I suggest, is a priority.

Utopian talk, you are thinking! Isn't the author aware of the *realities*? The threats to comprehensive education are more acute now than at any previous period over the last ten or twenty years. This is hardly the time to argue the case for developing the momentum towards comprehensive education – we are going to have a hard enough time simply defending what we've got. The whole system is under attack.

There is, of course, much truth in this assessment. But to my mind it doesn't prevent us holding in our minds a perspective – that of achieving a fully comprehensive system or systems for all to the age of eighteen – perhaps combining education with training. The actual process of defending existing systems may turn out to ignite yet again, in the present circumstances, a widespread and burning desire to complete the reform effectively – *and I mean effectively*. It may be that it is while the system is under attack that people come to realise its virtues. I think this is the lesson from past battles. As both Karl Marx and Robbie Burns said in their different ways – outcomes may be unexpected. The best laid plans of mice and men gang oft agley. The government's clear intentions may not be so easy to realise. The situation may be more complex than is dreamt of in their philosophy.

What are the present dangers to comprehensive education? They are several. I want here to focus only on structural issues. But before tangling with these concrete, practical and basically political questions, a few words are advisable on deeper questions underlying policy and practice.

Today, as regards the public provision of education, two principles stand opposed. The Education Act is fuelled by a certain ideology, that of the market place. Its progenitors put their faith in competition. Local financial management, open enrolment, grant maintained schools, even city technology colleges are all rationalised on the grounds that the resulting competitive battles for 'customers' between schools (seen almost as independent corporations) must inevitably result in the general improvement of educational practice and in the enhancement of standards. Good schools will drive out bad. Popular schools will expand, increase their prestige, flourish (some may even become independent), while 'unpopular' schools (mostly in fact in inner cities) will go into a spiral of decline, of low morale, and eventually, ceasing to be viable, will close. Such, at least, seems to be the desired scenario. So, according to this doctrine, and this must surely be an act of faith, overall, everything will get better. These conditions generally imply, as an essential part of this strategy, prising the schools loose from the local authorities. The chosen instruments to achieve this are the parents.

The other principle is the direct opposite of this. Its watchword is co-operation, rather than competition (though this does not exclude emulation, a more appropriate term, perhaps, when considering education). The principle, as I see it, is acceptance of responsibility for the equal provision of a public good – education, health or whatever. As Tawney once wrote, 'What the best and wisest parents want for their own children, the community must want for all its children.' Jackson Hall, ex-chair of the Society of Education Officers, in a recent, penetrating and critical article on local financial management in which he showed its potential for enhancing differentiation, put the matter quite clearly.[3] The local education authority has a responsibility for the provision of education *equally for all* – and the emphasis is on the words *for all*.

It may be there could be principled exceptions to this – and I mean *principled*; exceptions which can be defended and argued on rational grounds and which come to achieve general acceptance. An example might be a policy of positive discrimination, as advocated by Plowden, and implemented to some extent in the education priority areas, by which a higher than average proportion of available resources are allocated to particular groups of children in this case defined as deprived or disadvantaged. This would clearly be an exception to the principle of equal provision of resources. Before comprehensive reorganisation there used to be a generally accepted rational justification for the provision of greater resources to another specific group – those selected for grammar or technical schools. This found its rationale in the theory and practice of intelligence testing – that is, in arguments as to the supposed in-born, fixed and unchangeable nature of the child, and of differences between children which were held to be largely genetically determined and also accurately measurable. It was partly because this particular theory – or ideology, perhaps – had so strong a hold 30 or 40 years ago that the move to comprehensive education was delayed in this country compared, for instance to what happened in Sweden or Japan. But at least the issue was open to rational argument. When this ideology collapsed – and so failed to receive public support – the way was open for comprehensive education, and so to the *equal* provision of resources (which must be scarce) to all. But in fact this concept – that of equal provision of education as public good – was written into the 1944 Act, with its perspective of secondary education for all. On what other principle could the public provision of education find justification? Particularly in time of war, when equal sacrifices were demanded from all, and as freely given.

The market place philosophy which cannot, of course, lead to equality of provision and does not seek to, implies, as I have just suggested, loosening the malign grip (as some see it) of local authorities over their systems. It is now parents (as governors) who are to run the schools (though both David Hart and Kenneth Baker seem now to be saying it will be head teachers who undertake this function). Parents are thus counterposed, as a force, to local authorities. Schools are to become semi-independent corporate bodies (or small businesses). These must compete with each other in order to remain viable – and in a period over the immediate future of very sharply falling rolls in most areas. So the scene is set for the battles of the future.

Turning now to concrete practical issues arising from the Act, it is probable that the most immediate and potentially damaging threat to comprehensive systems lies in the provisions relating to grant maintained schools (or opting out) on the one hand, and to city technology colleges on the other. These together are intended to form the new third tier which Margaret Thatcher promised to construct in an interview in September 1987. 'You are going to have *three* systems,' she told the *Independent*. 'First there will be those who wish to stay with the local authority,' then 'You are going to have direct grant schools' funded directly by the state, 'and then you are going to have a private sector with assisted places'.[4]

These new types of school will provide the 'variety' that Kenneth Baker also promised.

These two initiatives both in their own way clearly represent threats to comprehensive systems. It seems, in considering the matter historically and I hope dispassionately, that policies of this kind were developed following the Solihull rebuff of 1984. Selection *between* schools, Keith Joseph then accepted in a television interview at the time, 'is largely out' – instead, he said, 'There must be differentiation *within* schools.'[5] But the policy in the Bill and Act has been developed since then. The problem for the government, it seems, was how to create the 'diversity' considered as a good in itself. Could not new types of schools be established which did not *directly* threaten the status of any existing school? Could not local systems be *circumvented* by the creation of new types? City technology colleges are a case in point. They could simply be added to local systems in a geographical sense, but be totally independent of them in their finance, their government and their accountability. If the impact on the local schools, particularly at a time of sharply falling rolls, was likely to be unhealthy (or, shall we say, unhelpful), well, what did that matter? So much the better, in a sense – destabilisation is needed to shake up the system. Competition is healthy, a good in itself – no matter that the competition is hardly between equals. More closures of 'bad' schools would be likely to follow. City technology colleges, it is argued in addition, could and would be *non-selective* on principle – though this hardly seems to square with practice in, for instance, the case of the CTC in Solihull where, after a massive propaganda drive with loudspeakers, glossy leaflets and the rest round the streets locally, applications certainly exceeded places. I note, incidentally, that the selective nature of this first CTC is now held up as a virtue by the Secretary of State himself. The Solihull school, he said approvingly recently, had been 'heavily over-subscribed' – 350 applications for 180 places.[6]

If the government now appears to be stressing the selectivity of CTC's as a virtue, this has not been the case as regards public pronouncements so far relating to grant maintained schools. These, it is claimed, will not breach present non-selective principles (I am referring of course to comprehensive schools, not grammar schools, which opt out). These schools will not be able to change their status for years, and then only after a lengthy procedure.[7] But in the real world, most people recognise that opted out schools will inevitably be subject to what is known as creeping selectivity. More important, perhaps, such schools will cease to be maintained by local authorities – cease to be an element in a local 'system'. This has, of course, enormous implications in terms of one of the authority's primary responsiblities – for planning, for ensuring, over the future, equal (or, at least, equitable) provision of a public good.

There are other features of the present scene which represent a threat to local systems. The Assisted Places Scheme, which has no serious justification today, is one of these. According to the

research study published recently, this scheme
certainly does not appear to have benefited deprived
but bright inner-city children, as was claimed by
responsible government spokesmen at the start as
the reason for its legitimacy.[8] This scheme could
well be expanded, as Margaret Thatcher suggested,
and of course it is a means of enhancing
privatisation of the school system. It could be used to
help grant maintained schools to become independent – this has already been hinted at, if not overtly
stated. Privatised 'educational' institutions are
certainly widely used, and encouraged, in the
provision of training for those aged between sixteen
and eighteen. So enhanced forms of privatisation,
which imply the removal of any form of democratic
control and accountability, remain a threat.

There is also, of course, a strong attack being
mounted against local authorities as such. This now
centres on the Hillgate group, but is certainly
represented at a high, perhaps the highest, level in
government. Sheila Lawlor's pamphlet entitled
Opting Out: A Guide to Why and How is full of what
reads like a paranoiac – or even pathological –
indignation and rage against local authorities. One
wonders sometimes where these people got their
experiences that make them so extraordinarily
vituperative. From the start it is assumed that we
all wish to be 'freed from the frustrations of local
authority interferences'; that we all agree that
schools are hindered 'by continual requests for
form-filling and interference from the town hall'.
That local authorities 'have, for too long, enjoyed a
monopoly control of vast education budgets'. That
many authorities 'have shown themselves at best
oblivious to the wishes of those whom they serve –
and at worst, callous in their contempt of them'; and

so on. If there have been cases lending credence to such outrageous judgements, who seriously maintains that these are characteristic of local government generally? This seems basically a case for psychotherapy.

Local government is the form that has evolved over the centuries into a system of democratic, and accountable, control over the provision of a wide variety of services, of which education is, of course, certainly the most important. We all know it has its weaknesses and crises, as does also central government. We all also know that its provision of services is not always done to perfection. I am not myself a local government man, in the sense that I have never worked directly in local government, either as an official or as an elected representative. But as an historian of education I have always felt that the contribution of local government has been severely underrated. Its record in the provision of education to local populations, while admittedly variegated, has been remarkable – very remarkable in some cases. It has thrown up outstanding Chief Education Officers, chairs of education committees, and the rest. It is not a dramatic form of public service, but it is an essential one; and it is nearer to the people than parliament and central government and recognised to be. We saw this very clearly in the massive support for the continuance of ILEA in the parent poll on its abolition – driven through parliament nevertheless. Some form of local government, I would argue, is essential for the provision of most public services and especially education. This does not mean that we should not think about how to improve structure and organisation – procedures. But it does mean that, if we want to retain comprehensive systems; or better, if we want a policy of 'a system of good schools' (as Briault advocated in his forgotten report on falling rolls),[9] then we need a form of expertly advised and democratically elected local government to plan and oversee the process and to negotiate with local populations and communities. My first conclusion, then, is that in the struggle to maintain progress towards a fully comprehensive system, local government should be retained and strengthened as its essential base in the locality, and that such authorities should retain powers of planning and monitoring the development of local systems. This is essential. (Their role cannot, or certainly should not, be reduced to monitoring the 'delivery' of the National Curriculum, as recently suggested by the Secretary of State.)

My second conclusion is that authorities, in co-operation with parents and their organisations, governors and their organisations, and community organisations of all kinds including the churches, need to unite to defend and extend their systems. Government representatives argue that the opting-out option, always available hereafter, will act to keep local authorities on their toes. Some local authority representatives make a rather similar set of points. For instance, in a recent article, Peter Cornall, ex-comprehensive head and now Chief Inspector for Cornwall, makes a series of concrete suggestions which, he believes, could demonstrate to local populations that education is still best provided through local government.[10] The Association of Metropolitan Authorities is said to be preparing a campaign having similar objectives. It seems to me that it may now be possible to create a fairly dense protective (or defensive) structure around local authority systems of schools, and so to develop a kind of unified ethos and perspective which could be of advantage generally in extending and developing comprehensive systems. I know some authorities have taken active steps in this direction over the last year or so. If this results in real community and parental support for local systems, that would be one definite and valuable gain from all these events.

We must not, however, underestimate the challenge. The government has shown a certain steely purpose about this Bill (or Act) from the start, as we know well. This was shown first in the decision not to pay any serious attention whatever to the original 'consultation' process sparked by the issue of the main consultation papers last summer. It was shown also in the inflexibility displayed by the government in the proceedings in Parliament. In this connection Lord Hailsham's comment about an 'elective dictatorship' has been revived in a new context. In the Commons Committee, so far as I know, not a single concession of any value was gained from the long hours of debate; and this goes also for the debates on the second and third readings in the full Commons. Expected revolts by back-bench Tory MPs never materialised – or were effectively contained. The Bill then went to the Lords virtually unaltered. Although several doughty battles were fought there (where the Committee was of the full House), little of importance was achieved – at least as regards the schools clauses – the main issues with which I am concerned. The compromise on religious education achieved there is tangential to the issues we are concerned with; as also the minor changes won on higher education relating to academic freedom, tenure and funding. The only important modification gained concerned opting-out procedures, said to have been due to an outbreak of salmonella poisoning which seemed selectively to have attacked government supporters in greater numbers than the opposition – an act of God, perhaps. And this defeat, though then modified in the Commons, has led to a minor, but perhaps important, change in the relevant section of the Act, concerning the requirement for a second ballot if less than 50 per cent of parents vote at the initial poll. So, basically, the Bill or Act, while enormously expanded (Peter Wilby's description of it as a 'Gothic Monstrosity' seems very appropriate) has remained in its original form, at least as concerns the schools, except of course for the abolition of the ILEA which was the result of an unexpected raid by Norman Tebbit and Michael Heseltine in the Commons. Attempts to secure a pause for reconsideration of this item was voted down in the Lords with the help of the mobilisation of backwoods peers on a huge scale, paralleling the similar mobilisation against Lord Chelwood's amendment asking for a similar pause and re-think of the poll tax.

The government is, then, showing a steely purpose with this legislation, and it is likely that every effort will be made to exploit to the full the new possibilities in line with free market thinking and ideology. So, immediately after the Bill's passage (or even earlier) we have the establishment of a so-called independent unit or 'trust' to assist schools wishing, or considering, the opting out option.[11] Already (in August 1988) glossy documents have been circulated to all relevant primary and secondary schools apparently extolling the merits of grant maintained status. This unit is known to have semi-official status and backing. The government's steely purpose has surely also been made abundantly clear in the last few days in the whole mix-up about governing bodies, where the attempt to rush through their reconstitution seems likely to run into legal difficulties.[12] Of course, actions of this kind ideally have to be undertaken carefully, or tactfully. No one likes to feel he or she is being browbeaten. But the pressure is clearly on, and will be intensified.

Those who wish to preserve and develop their local comprehensive system have a perfect constitutional right, it seems to me, to counter propaganda or activities of this kind in whatever ways they find most effective. But such action needs to get off the ground as early as possible. In relation to the passage of this Bill, the speed of action of the government has been a distinctive feature, and we had better get used to it. Those who oppose the Act's objectives – who are resistant, shall we say, to 'new realism' and they are many, as expressed during its passage – need to be *as active* in ensuring the legitimate defence of their systems, even if the pressure has semi-official support. The Act gives governing bodies the right to apply to opt out. It also gives them the right not so to act. Active support for either of these standpoints is absolutely legitimate. This needs to be made abundantly clear to all. The case for the defence of local systems of comprehensive education needs to be put at least as strongly and effectively as the alternative, if possible, more so.

As regards the city technology colleges – here the case is different. The initiative to set up such colleges does not rest with local authorities in any way or sense. It rests apparently with the Secretary of State, since a section of the Act specifically legitimates these colleges – and permits finance from the Exchequer to be used both for capital costs

and recurrent expenditure, though initially it was
hoped all capital costs would be born by industry. In
spite of this change, Kenneth Baker last week
claimed that 'the government has had more support
for City Technology Colleges than for any other
venture this century' – this hyperbole seems
unbelievable. Further it is common knowledge that
it does not square with the facts.[13]

Here again, another semi-official body or trust,
publicly funded, has been established to press
forward in all sorts of ways with this initiative. So
we need to assess realistically the degree of
determination being shown here also, in spite of the
breakdown of the original plans for industrial
support. But few authorities, whatever their
political complexion, are likely to welcome a CTC in
their area. And I believe very few have (though it
seems that Solihull is once more an exception).
Whatever may be the case for the establishment of
such institutions (and I do not believe that a credible
case has yet been made), few authorities could easily
assimilate such a cuckoo's egg in its nest without
serious disruption of its existing system of secondary education. This is a major objection to this
initiative. Many hold that the money to be made
available for financing these colleges (actually
schools), most of which it is now clear will come from
the Exchequer, would be far better spent in
resourcing rather more effectively the existing
schools for the mass of ordinary children. And
incidentally, if these schools really do imply a return
to selection (as seems probable and as seems desired
by the government) – then it seems odd that we are
the only advanced industrial country in the entire
world (so far as I know) seriously planning such a
return, if by these devious routes.

Almost immediately the Act received Royal Assent a ban was imposed on all reorganisation proposals with the DES (as well as others, of course, planned to go in). The object of this 'planning blight' (as Gordon Cunningham had described it) appears to be precisely to allow schools threatened (if that is the right word) with reorganisation to apply for grant maintained status in order to remain as they are. Hence the undignified rush and pressure for the reconstitution of governing bodies, since a time limit for this blight clearly had to be set.

This action is, in my view, sharp and exceptionally aggressive – indeed it could almost be described in terms of sabotage of local systems. It seems an extraordinary act for the state to take, since the state, or in this case the government, has overall responsibility for the *health* and *effective functioning* of the nation's educational system as a whole. Rationalisation of local systems is absolutely necessary, as the government's own Audit Commission frequently points out. I know that various honeyed words have been said – denials issued, and so on. But surely it is clear to all that the desire of individual schools to maintain their sixth forms, for instance, is to be used as the means of persuading them to apply for grant maintained status. That is obvious.

The fact is that it has become a *political imperative* to make a success of these sections of the Act, as we all know very well indeed. Reputations, and futures, will depend on it. But who is counting the cost for the children in those systems whose leading schools will have been prised loose? It is the overall impact of these individual decisions in specific areas that needs to be assessed, if we are to approach this question in what might be called a statesmanlike manner. This approach now seems conspicuously absent from official actions. This makes it more important than ever that local authorities, and others supporting the continued existence and development of viable (I repeat, viable) comprehensive systems, ensure that local populations are kept *fully informed* as to the issues at stake. It is likely that intentions can only be thwarted if a sufficient head of steam can be generated locally in opposition to actions that may appear both cynical and irresponsible.

Education officers, heads, teachers, members of governing bodies, councillors and educational administrators generally need now to recall that comprehensive secondary education was originally very much a local authority based, grass roots movement, strongly supported by teachers and others who saw in this transition one to a more humane, more flexible, more sensible school system than that we were left with in the late 1940s and early 1950s. Central government did not *in any way* lend support to burgeoning local comprehensive systems before the issue of Circular 10/65 (in 1965, of course); and even then the running continued to be left to local authorities – not the government itself. The first post-war Labour government has had a bad press in the main historical studies recently published precisely for its conservatism in education. It actively imposed the tripartite system, making exceptions only for those areas which had a certain political clout and a good deal of stubborn determination. I refer primarily to the old London County Council, Middlesex at times, the West Riding, later Coventry and one or two other areas. These made the running in the late 1940s and early 1950s. Then the great industrial cities of the north took over – Liverpool, Manchester, Sheffield, Bradford – the roll call could be greatly extended – all expressed their *determination* to transform their systems well before 10/65. All faced central obstruction and difficulties – though this was relaxed when Edward Boyle felt strong enough to give muted support in 1963-64. We can recall the great administrators of that period – Graham Savage of London (still I believe, though over 90, supportive and involved); Stewart Mason of Leicestershire, who brought what was in fact almost a feudal county into the forefront of educational progress – the first English county to achieve overall reorganisation in 1969 – and Alec Clegg of the West Riding. Both Mason and Clegg, incidentally, were also much concerned with primary education, with the arts, music and drama. Then we should recall the great heads of the whole saga. Trevor Lovett of Holyhead, a highly professional schoolmaster, head of the first genuine comprehensive in England and Wales, back in the late 1940s or early 1950s. Sir William Cretney of Castle Rushen in the Isle of Man – the first comprehensive Knight! Raymond King, who guided the transformation of Wandsworth Grammar School to comprehensive status – a strong supporter of comprehensive education even during the war itself when he, and three other then well-known grammar school heads, known in Gordon Square (headquarters of the Incorporated Association of Head Masters) as 'the four horsemen of the Apocalypse', strongly embraced the concept of the single school, agitated for it, and in Raymond's case finally brought it into being within his own school through its extension to include a non-selective intake. Margaret Miles (Dame), who did the same in London also, transforming Putney High

School into Mayfield comprehensive – one of the most advanced and well organised schools of the period.

There are many others, heroes and heroines of the movement who deserve celebration. But that is not the point. The point is to recall the historical record, what may accurately be called the Great Tradition. These experiences are there for all to draw on. It is not likely, I believe, that we will turn our backs on this tradition, and tamely succumb to new initiatives, from whatever source, which threaten to destroy this heritage. Experience already shows, as indicated at the start, that consciousness of the value of what has been achieved has bitten too deeply into the minds of ordinary people up and down the country, who fight to defend their schools and school systems when they are threatened, and usually do so successfully.

It is in this spirit, I believe, that we should approach the challenges of today. Challenges are no bad thing, if they force a rethink and a reconstruction of practices which may have become ingrained, routine and obsolete. I personally believe that comprehensive education was subjected to a largely unjustified campaign of abuse and denigration in the late 1970s and early 1980s almost unexampled in the history of education. The criticism, as many have pointed out, coincided almost precisely with a sharp economic and financial crisis which hit the country when oil prices quadrupled in 1973. From that period our schools have suffered and, although there have been many positive developments and new thinking, there have been no clear goals and objectives enunciated by those in authority – often, rather, a painful rejection or denial of responsibility, as we saw for four or five years recently. Now the situation has changed. Now there does at last seem to be some readiness to credit achievements or even to claim them when they are disputable. HMI and DES reactions to GCSE results recently are a case in point – there have been others too.

One thing is clear. The transformation of education in this country cannot be brought about by edict, nor even by Act of Parliament. It requires the active co-operation of *all* those involved – but especially the teachers, local authorities and their officials, advisers, parents and governors. Outcomes, as I suggested earlier can be unexpected. Perhaps from all the trauma of the last year, and more, something good will emerge. I hope so. The opportunity is there if we can seize it. Provided always we do not relax, even for a single instant. But continue to monitor everything with eagle eyes. And react accordingly and according to principle.

Notes and References

1. Robert Dunn, *Education*, 8 July 1988.
2. Quoted in Brian Simon, *Education and the Social Order, 1940-1990*, London 1991, p. 448.
3. Jackson Hall, 'Directed to the Wrong Church', *Times Educational Supplement*, 5 August 1988.
4. *Independent*, 14 September 1987.
5. *Times Educational Supplement*, 17 February 1984.
6. *Independent*, 5 September 1988.
7. This condition has been abrogated recently by Kenneth Clarke; see pp. 165-6. [Note added September 1991.]
8. As very clearly shown in a recent research study, Tony Edwards, John Fitz and Geoff Whitty, *The State and Private Education: an Evaluation of the Assisted Places Scheme*, London 1989.
9. Eric Briault and Frances Smith, *Falling Rolls in the Secondary Schools*, Parts I and II, London 1980.
10. Peter Cornall, 'Guaranteed Curriculum, Locally Grown', *Forum*, Vol.31, No.1, Autumn 1988.
11. For this unit, see p. 58.
12. See p. 65.
13. *Independent*, 5 September 1988.

3 Thatcher's Third Tier, or Bribery and Corruption*

The main purposes of the 1988 Education Act were made abundantly clear at the start. First, to break the power of the local authorities which traditionally had been directly responsible for running their own 'systems' of education, and second, to erect (or reinforce) an hierarchical system of schooling both subject to market forces and more directly under central state control. The contradiction inherent within this latter objective is well encapsulated in Thatcher's definition of the proposed new sub-system as comprising 'state independent schools'.

This chapter is concerned with the deliberate creation of a new system of schools between the independent ('public' and private) schools for the better-off, and the remnants of local authority schools for the masses left with the local authorities. This new 'system', independent of the local authorities, state-financed, but partially subject to market forces, is designed (according to ministerial pronouncements) to increase choices available to parents and (in the case of city technology colleges) to institutionalise new approaches to the curriculum. The means by which this new, third system is to be created is both through the establishment of

* First published in May 1990.

city technology colleges (CTCs) and, through the opting out sections of the Act, the establishment of the so-called grant maintained schools (GMSs).

Both types of school are to be directly funded by the state through the DES, even if CTCs derive some of their initial capital funds from industry and GMSs current expenditure is clawed back from the local authorities.[1] Both will be overseen (though how is not yet clear) by the central authority. Both are to be, in a constitutional, managerial and financial sense, entirely independent of the local authority in whose area they are situated. By these means, new systems of schools are to be brought into being under the ultimate control of the central, rather than the local authority. The objective of equal provision of a public good (education) under local democratic control is hereby rejected.

To master-mind, and enhance, the thrust from the centre to establish this new sub-system, new power foci have been created; and indeed the speed with which this has been done is notable. First (though not necessarily chronologically) the City Technology Colleges Trust was established, privately funded, having as its main purpose the furthering of the (faltering) cause of the city technology colleges. In addition a specific unit has been established at the DES, employing sixteen officials at a cost of £300,000 a year, to provide advice and services normally the responsibility of the local authority. The trust's chairman is Cyril Taylor, knighted recently 'for services to education'. Its chief executive is Susan Frey. Since its foundation it has energetically pursued its objective, with what results we will assess later.

Second, the Grant Maintained Schools Trust was also brought into being, in this case actually before

the 1988 Act received Royal Assent. It was ready and
running immediately after, and circulated all
governing bodies and school heads already in August
1988 with a glossy brochure inviting schools to opt
out. Its dual function then was firstly to 'assist'
schools to opt out (for this function the trust was privately funded – by industry), and secondly to service
schools which had opted out (for this, they needed
government funds). A year later, in October 1989, this
organisation split into two, the objective being to
qualify for charitable status specifically to assist the
second of these functions. There are now, therefore,
two separate organisations (although they share the
same office). The first, Choice in Education Ltd, the
director of which is Andrew Turner, now undertakes
the propaganda function involving persuasion. The
other, the GMS trust, which now has an application in
for charitable status, derives its resources both from
industry and from the DES, which has made substantial grants towards its work.[2]

All four organisations have official blessing – or (as
with the CTC unit) are part of the DES and responsible to its Ministers. Their activities are by now a
familiar aspect of the current educational scene.
They are a clear sign, to the world of education and
beyond, as to where the government's main interests
lie – at least as far as the school system is concerned.
Their presence and activity clearly underline the
main thrust of government policy: the lack of any
kind of vibrant concern with the great majority of the
nation's schools, distaste for the local authorities
within whose systems these exist, faith in the new
'beacons of excellence'. Ministerial pronouncements
consistently emphasise the success and pioneering
achievements of these two sets of schools, even if the
first of these have only recently come into being.

City Technology Colleges

We may first assess the situation relating to this initiative. It is well known that industry in general has been distinctly unenthusiastic, preferring to siphon what money they are prepared to give in support of schools to quite other projects (such as the various compacts now being developed). The result has been that the bulk of the finance needed to get CTCs off the ground has been contributed by the tax-payer, through the Treasury. Then, because the initial expenses of creating new schools were greatly under-estimated (MacGregor has put the blame on his civil servants), costs rapidly escalated, so that the Treasury (apparently) called a halt. The target is now defined as limited to completion of the plan for twenty such 'Colleges' first announced by Kenneth Baker to the Conservative Party conference in October 1986. Such, at least officially, appears to be the objective, but matters are more complex than that, as we shall see.

The cost to the Exchequer for these twenty schools is put at £135 million for the three years 1990-91 to 1992-93 (in the January public expenditure White Paper). To this should be added the sum already spent of £35 million, making a total of £170 million. For this the tax-payer will get twenty schools of about 1,000 pupils each. Plans, as I write, are uncertain. The CTC trust claims three schools now open (Solihull in 1988, Nottingham and Middlesbrough in 1989), five to open this year (1990) at Bradford, Gateshead, Dartford, Norwood (London), and Croydon (the BRIT 'Fame' school – but this date is now reported as abandoned in this case); six in 1991 at Surrey Docks (London), Corby, Lewisham (London), East Brighton, Telford and in Glasgow (the 'Scottish Technology Academy'). This gives a total of fourteen – a shortfall of six. In November 1989 Angela Rumbold, however, announced that, in addition to the existing three such schools, eight now had firm opening dates this year and next – a total of eleven, adding that five companies or individuals were prepared for major participation.[3] If all these latter emerge successfully as colleges, the total reaches sixteen: a shortfall of four. The target of twenty seems not, as yet, to have been effectively secured, although, as I write, another CTC appears to have been 'parachuted in' at Wandsworth. To date, contributions from industry are claimed to have reached some £45 million. However Mrs Rumbold has announced that the next seven CTCs will receive 80 per cent of their cash from the tax-payer, 20 per cent from industry.

The procedures used by the CTC trust to establish colleges have created consternation throughout the country. These activities are, perhaps, best likened to those of the Barbary pirates in the Mediterranean in the late eighteenth century. Consultation with local authorities seems non-existent; instead, sudden announcements are made when a scheme, secretly negotiated, reaches fruition, usually leading to immediate and strong protests in the areas involved, which now find themselves caught up in this power play.

This, for instance, was the case at Telford, where the Shropshire LEA, which first heard of the proposition through the media, had carried through a sixth form reorganisation plan precisely in the area chosen – a CTC, it was reported, could have 'a devastating effect' on the secondary schools in Telford, as well as those at Shrewsbury and Bridgnorth.[4] The Steiner school proposed near

Brighton (a 'cloak and dagger plan') is reported as having generated 'intense ill-will among almost every local interest you could think of' – the initiative was regarded as politically motivated.[5] A proposal for a college at Walsall has met with the local council's 'fundamental objection' to any such attempt due to falling rolls and other factors; such an initiative, it was claimed, would certainly lead to the closure of a local school.[6] And anger boiled over at Wandsworth, as is well known, when the establishment of two CTCs was suddenly announced, together with other already controversial initiatives (magnet schools). This reached a high point at the end of January 1990 when the heads of all the secondary schools in Wandsworth signed a letter to the press protesting about these procedures. This was followed by a vote of no confidence in their Chief Education Officer by all the head-teachers in the borough – an unprecedented event.[7] The 'Fame' school at Croydon, whose future seems highly uncertain (if it has one at all), has also been the target of well organised local protests, thereby losing the support of many of its initial (and well-known) patrons.[8] Some of the developments have been unsavoury – perhaps particularly the ADT (a security and car auction business) initiative first at Barnet, then at Wandsworth, where the sponsors switched direction in search of 'a fast bang for its bucks' as one of them put it. Here also the political advantages to be gained appeared clearly as a major factor in the sponsor's plans.[9] It is this kind of thing that has brought the charge of corruption against this whole initiative.

In spite of all this, the trust is pushing on regardless. Political reputations depend on success, as has been made abundantly clear from the start.

There is a clear determination to carry the plan through whatever the difficulties – to sweep local opposition aside. Strong passions are aroused – and not surprisingly. The January expenditure White Paper made it abundantly clear that, over the next three years, a substantial cut is to be made in educational expenditure; though some extra money is to be provided for higher education, the schools generally are to suffer yet further stringency. But with one exception. Large sums, as we have seen, are to be made available for city technology colleges.[10]

In these circumstances it is not surprising that those concerned directly with maintaining viable school systems are becoming increasingly critical. This was very clearly expressed by Andrew Collier, Lancashire's CEO and this year's President of the Society of Education Officers (SEO). In his Presidential address to the Society towards the end of January, Collier described CTCs as 'a criminal waste of money'. 'Let us waste no more of our energies on twenty experimental schools,' he said, 'when there is so much to be done with more than 27,000 maintained schools, which really do have a major effect on the future generation.'[11] MacGregor, who spoke later to the same conference, responded emotionally to this critique which, in some ways, was unprecedented.

Collier was giving expression to what was becoming a generally held view among those responsible for local systems. A few weeks earlier Tim Brighouse, until recently CEO for Oxfordshire, characterised CTCs as 'unfair', not needed and a waste of money (at the annual North of England conference). Jack Straw, who from the start has opposed this initiative, also at this time characterised CTCs as 'a criminal waste of money', adding, 'but a deeply corrupt one as well'. Angela Rumbold, on the other hand, claimed that the 'CTC programme' was 'making excellent progress'.[12]

The intention ultimately to extend the programme well beyond the original twenty colleges had been made clear officially even before the last election. Robert Dunn, then junior minister, had stated that the aim was not twenty, but 220, perhaps 420 such colleges. Cost limitations are now proving a difficulty. But early in the New Year new possibilities were pursued by Cyril Taylor of the CTC Trust. Already last October the *Independent* reported that Taylor had spoken about 'hundreds' of CTCs, but these would be 'funded by LEAs'. In December the *Guardian* reported a nationwide city college plan was likely, suggesting that plans to establish at least one in each of the 104 LEAs was expected soon to be announced. The plan was to persuade authorities to convert existing schools to CTCs. 'We are optimistic', said Cyril Taylor, 'that for modest sums the programme can be considerably expanded.' The cost of conversion would be as little as £1 million per school.[13] This plan implies taking existing schools out of local control and handing them over to industry since the sponsors determine governing bodies.

A plan of this sort took concrete form with the proposal to convert an existing voluntary-aided comprehensive school in Wandsworth to a CTC (Battersea Park). ADT pledged the required 15 per cent of the cost. Here was a new possible road ahead. Sir Cyril Taylor was reported as 'jubilant'. He had argued for two years that the voluntary-aided route 'would open the flood gates for CTCs', since the schools were already up and running and costs to industry were minimal. 'Better sixteen voluntary-aided that one orthodox college.' This would give

CTCs 'the breakthrough the trust needs into the local authority system'.[14] Talks were now reported relating to the creation of eleven more CTCs with Kent, other local authorities and church authorities.[15] Apparently this conversion is legally acceptable, even though the vast majority of voluntary-aided schools are church schools (the category was specifically established to meet their needs). Such a break-through, of course, would require local authority and usually church support and co-operation. But what appears to be intended is to bring about, through exploitation of the voluntary-aided category, a major educational change. The possibility of some degree of success here – given support of such initiatives by this government – should not be underestimated (for later developments in this area see pp. 170-1).

Opting Out – Grant Maintained Schools

CTCs are one prong of the attack – the other, of course, is embodied in the opting out sections of the Act. What is the position here?

In September 1989 the 18 schools which had gained grant maintained status in the first year following the passage of the Act began to operate as such. Two months later (early November 1989) a further ten had had their applications accepted, and by mid-January 1990 the total approved (including the original eighteen) had reached 32. Nine schools had had their applications rejected, but another seventeen were, at this time, still awaiting decision by the Secretary of State.[16] One factor already stood out very clearly. The bulk of the schools voting to opt out were schools subject to reorganisation proposals by local authorities seeking to rationalise provision, especially in the light of falling rolls.[17] These were all schools threatened (if that is the right word) with amalgamation, closure, or some other change of status consequent upon reorganisation. Very few were opting out from a clear desire to go independent of the local authority.

It will be remembered that Kenneth Baker imposed what has been called a 'planning blight' on the consideration by the DES of local authority reorganisation proposals for five months immediately following the passage of the Act (see p. 51). This was specifically done to ensure that the new governing bodies (under the 1986 Act) might consider the alternative of applying for grant maintained status.[18] By that means, in effect, the country's entire system was frozen for five months in the pursuit of the government's objectives relating to local authority 'systems'. Since then, while the Audit Commission (and even government ministers) have continued to press the need for rationalisation on local authorities, the same over-riding factor (preservation of individual schools subject to reorganisation plans) has dominated the opting out scheme. After a series of harsh experiences, authorities have to all intents and purposes ceased to submit (and plan) reorganisation schemes, since a single school so 'threatened' can disrupt plans covering an entire authority.

This has happened in several cases. In Tameside, for instance, Tony Webster, the CEO, protested to MacGregor early in November 1989, following such a decision, that the authority's plan to take 1,500 places out of use, so enabling the authority to concentrate its resources on the remaining schools, was totally negated by his decision to allow the school proposed for closure to become grant maintained. Not only was the authority unable to implement the plan, wrote the CEO, but the continued expense of surplus places in the authority's area was by, this action, guaranteed.[19] At this moment also Gloucestershire protested that the decision of Downfields school in Stroud to apply to opt out would, if accepted, undermine the county's reorganisation plan for the area and squander public money.[20] In Bedfordshire it was claimed (by the chair of the Education Committee) that the permission given (by Baker) to allow Queensbury School in Dunstable to opt out had paralysed all rational planning. This school had been selected for closure to provide viability for two remaining upper schools, having the smallest intake and weakest staying on rate of the three. Closure would have saved £900,000 through the removal of 1,000 surplus places. Following this experience, the council decided not to put up any further closure plans for another four years, 'given that the government can incite any such school with more than 300 pupils to go it alone'.[21] In January this year Derbyshire were also forced to abandon plans to get rid of 1,000 places when a former grammar school whose closure was central to the scheme, opted out.[22]

By this time a real planning blight had once again descended on the system throughout the country. This extraordinary policy (is the Audit Commission calculating its actual cost?) appeared to be reinforced by MacGregor's decision to allow Beechen Cliff boys school in Bath to opt out. The authority's proposal was that this school be closed in phases from 1991 and turned into a sixth form college, the city's remaining schools switching from eleven-to-eighteen to eleven-to-sixteen schools. This proposal has been hammered out in a two year's long public consultation process and was widely supported. MacGregor, however, negated the entire scheme by his decision which, indeed, now threw Bath's reorganisation into chaos.[23]

At last, at this stage, a local authority took the issue to a judicial review in the High Court and, as is well known, MacGregor's decision relating to Beechen Cliff was quashed by the judge, who ordered the minister to reconsider both proposals (the local authority plan and the opting out application). In his judgement, Mr Justice Hutchison said that 'it could not have been the intention of Parliament, in drawing up the opting-out legislation, to allow education reorganisation schemes to be undermined, and effectively frustrated, by permitting schools facing closure under such proposals to acquire grant maintained status'.[24] But that is precisely what has been happening in different local authority areas up and down the country over the whole of the last 18 months and more.

It is too early to assess the significance, and outcome, of the Avon judgement, but at the very least it seems likely that what has been to date the main factor motivating schools to opt out may now have reduced force. Only the future can show. But at this stage new factors have entered the scene. There is a good deal of evidence that disproportionate financial incentives are now being dangled before the schools in a further effort to promote opting out. This takes two forms.

First, the 18 schools which obtained grant maintained status last September have received their financial allocations for the year. The amount allotted exceeds their actual cost under LEA funding by an average of as much as 18 per cent. As part of their propaganda, Choice in Education Ltd. has produced a chart giving striking visual confirmation of this excess. The extra money these schools are to get represents their share of the local authority's central services, now allotted directly to the schools. Of course some of them may have to buy back some of these services out of this money. But probably not all. For instance local inspection or advisory services need not be bought back, since it is now (apparently) no one's job to monitor educational developments (or quality) in opted out schools. Nevertheless the GMS school's share of these services is still allotted to the schools.

Some would regard this as sharp practice. Others as simple bribery. However it is assessed there is now clearly a financial incentive, in terms of annual running costs, favouring the decision to opt out. But this is by no means all – there is also the question of capital costs.

These were announced in January. They show extraordinary variations. Colyton Grammar school in Devon was allotted £826,000. St James C of E at Bolton £667,000. Bacup and Rawtenstall Grammar school in Lancashire gained £640,000. Audenshawe High school, Tameside, was allotted £592,400 – 'We're quids in, we all know we are,' announced the head of the school triumphantly.[25] If these were the most favoured schools, the average capital allocation for all the GMS schools in fact amounted to £276,000 while the average for 25,000 schools in the country as a whole was £15,000.[26] Commenting on this allocation, the *Times Educational Supplement* said that 'the disproportionate capital sums lavished on GMS schools have been justified (by the DES, BS) on the grounds that these schools have been neglected', but when the Inspectorate finds (in its January report on the state of the schools) that two out of three secondary schools in the country as a whole are in an unsatisfactory condition 'it becomes apparent that opting out does indeed earn preferential treatment'.[27]

Conclusion

Clearly a powerful thrust is now being made, by the Government and its agencies, to ensure success both for opting out, and for completion (or extension) of the CTC programme. No holds are barred in this battle. Financial incentives, honours, evasion of statutory duties (or 'bending the rules') – all these and more are being thrown into the ring. What is at stake is not only the future of local government as a whole – this is threatened in more ways than this; what is at stake is the entire objective of providing equally for all – the essential function of the local authority, as many emphasise today. There is now a determined effort, of which the tactics discussed in this article form only a part, to destroy the school system in the form that it actually exists, and to substitute a new situation (hardly a 'system') where market forces not only predominate, but, through this very predominance, gradually enhance inequality of provision as deliberate policy. Polarisation of schools locally, through open entry, the opt out option, and so on, is planned to reflect polarisation within society, recently graphically underlined.[28] To achieve this involves removing control over local systems from the local authority – this is the means to a greater prize. The ideological legitimisation for the new order is found in the doctrine of parental choice – and related to that, of parent power.

While recognising that parents must have greater say within the school system, their first concern, as parents, is to their own children, and then to the individual school these attend. So parents can be led to fight to remove schools from local control if they believe that, by this means, they will do better for their own children – the cost to others is not, by this mechanism, taken into account. But who, then suffers? And who looks after these? By setting their objectives to provide equally for all, this is the function of the local authority, democratically elected by the population as a whole. That is why developments such as those discussed in this article must be seen for what they are: attempts to switch the whole thrust of the existing system in a quite new direction, towards ensuring unequal provision for those already advantaged within society as a whole.

This is not only an ungenerous objective; it is profoundly anti-human in its implications. At the same time, the means being used to ensure its success are contemptible.

Notes and References

1. See Brian Simon, *Bending the Rules*, London 1988, pp. 69ff.
2. Information in this paragraph from Mr Andrew Turner.
3. *Education*, 3 November 1989.
4. Ibid., 14 July 1989.
5. Nicholas Bagnall, 'College of Advanced Controversy', *Independent*, 9 November 1989.
6. *Education*, 24 November 1989.
7. Ibid., 19 January 1990; 2 February 1990; 16 February 1990.
8. See the *Times*, 30 November 1989, and especially Simon Gawfield, 'Off-stage Disarray Threatens "Fame" School's Debut', *Independent on Sunday*, 11 February 1990.
9. *Education*, 19 January 1990; 2 February 1990; *Independent*, 29 January 1990.
10. *Times Educational Supplement*, 2 February 1990; *Independent*, 31 January 1990.
11. *Education*, 26 January 1990.

12. *Times Educational Supplement*, 12 January 1990; *Independent*, 31 January 1990; *Education*, 3 November 1989.
13. *Independent*, 7 October 1989; *Guardian*, 4 December 1989.
14. *Times Educational Supplement*, 19 January 1990; 12 January 1990.
15. *Education*, 19 January 1990.
16. Information from Grant Maintained Schools Trust.
17. This applies to 23 of the first 33 applications, *Times Educational Supplement*, 2 December 1988.
18. See Brian Simon, op. cit., 3rd (revised) edition, November 1988, pp. 177-78.
19. *Education*, 10 November 1989.
20. Ibid., 10 November 1989.
21. *Times*, 2 October 1989, article by David Grugeon.
22. *Times Educational Supplement*, 12 January 1990.
23. Ibid., 12 January 1990.
24. *Independent*, 24 February 1990.
25. *Education*, 2 February 1990 (capital allocations); *Independent*, 2 February 1990.
26. *Times Educational Supplement*, 2 February 1990.
27. Ibid., 9 February 1990.
28. A. H. Halsey (ed.), *British Social Trends since 1900* (1988 edn.), pp. 26-33.

4 The National Curriculum, School Organisation and the Teacher*

I want to start with a few general, but very personal, impressions. My own engagement with Lawrence Stenhouse – and the very unusual and stimulating team around him, from whom, to my mind, he is inseparable – began when Jean Rudduck invited me, at an early British Educational Research Association (BERA) conference at Westfield College in London, to act as external examiner for the full-time MA – then the only teaching commitment at the Centre for Applied Research in Education (CARE) at the University of East Anglia. This team, from the Humanities Curriculum Project, was of course funded (or, more accurately, I believe, partially funded) specifically as a research unit (in 'Applied Research') at UEA – itself a highly imaginative move masterminded, I believe by Geoffrey Caston; the sort of thing that was still possible in the expansionist early 1970s when some of those in authority were still prepared to search out and encourage imaginative and innovative thinkers and practitioners and, in a sense, to give them their head.

There is perhaps no better way of penetrating into

* Delivered as a paper in August 1990.

the inner thinking, outlook, emphases, relationships within an educational institution than that of acting as external examiner – especially if the students whose work is being evaluated is a relatively small group whose studies can be made available. Indeed this stint lasted many years since, when it was completed for the full-time MA, a part-time equivalent had been started and I undertook this also. Of course I shall reveal no secrets (indeed I have none). But though I came from what might be called a progressive and in some respects an innovative institution – the School of Education at the University of Leicester – each time I took the road to Norwich I knew I was entering a different world. Lawrence argues somewhere that the central focus for educational studies must be education itself, its processes and practice – not, for instance, psychology, philosophy, history, sociology, even if all these have something to offer. This approach (of Lawrence's) may not now sound so original, and this is, perhaps a measure of advance, but at that time (fifteen to twenty years ago) to find an MA course which focused so specifically on the schools, their curricula and organisation, their relations with the external world; on the processes of teaching and learning within the classroom and the school as a whole; on staff relationships and their influence on procedures, patterns and outlook; on local authority involvement and its effect – all this was to me at least, a complete eye-opener and, more than that, extremely refreshing. Not only that, but the new techniques of research and study being developed, many of which arose out of the team's own research studies, and which owed a good deal to the developing 'Illuminative' paradigm (an issue hotly argued of course), ensured a rigorous research discipline underlying the new investigative approaches. The result can best be described as a new empowerment of the teachers who, of course, formed the large majority of the students. The more long term product, one could reasonably expect and hope for, was the actual improvement of practice – that is, better schools (which is also a fundamental objective of BERA, being written into its constitution).

But it was not only the content of the work and studies actually achieved which was impressive. There was also the question of relationships – particularly among the staff and students – all adult of course. I can't attempt to define this except perhaps to say that it contained nothing of the *de haut en bas* element not unusual in universities. Relationships were as between equals, involving mutual respect for the different knowledge, experience and expertise of the teacher-students on the one hand, and the teacher-staff on the other. Both, of course, were primarily and fundamentally involved in research activities. In a very real sense these relationships presented a paradigm of what all educational institutions should aspire to.

Perhaps I have said enough to indicate why, as I regularly, for over twelve years, left Leicester for the flat lands to the East I felt a sense of excitement – even of liberation. This achievement was, of course, that of the whole team that originally formed CARE, and of their later helpers. Indeed the historian of education, interested in networks and their influence, is bound in the long run to trace out the origins and development of the CARE network, now widespread not only in Britain but across the English-speaking world generally and elsewhere as well. This network stands for very definite values and procedures, values which, I suggest, accrue an enhanced significance with every year that passes.

This is why, at this particular moment in time, it is especially important to recall, and to consider afresh, the main thrust of Lawrence's teaching and consequent procedures. But this is a subjective undertaking, and I must immediately add, 'as I understand them'; and I do so diffidently, partly because of my own lack of direct involvement in the curriculum reform movement of the late 1960s and later, in which Lawrence played so crucial a role.

What is the position that the schools face today? We have a National Curriculum, defined and reinforced by statute – but it is already in disarray. This is based on a subject and on an objectives model – both rejected in no uncertain terms by Lawrence himself in a closely reasoned analysis. Modifications, or various measures introduced or announced over the last year seem to indicate that, perhaps unsurprisingly, the traditional objective of enhancing differentiation is being pursued with some vigour: three separate sciences in GCSE (to cater specifically for the independent and top state schools), 20 per cent science for some; 12.5 per cent for the rest – the established three-fold division raises its head once again even in the new dispensation. Then there are the continuous indications of back-tracking as regards the scope of the curriculum – particularly ominous, perhaps, being the official proposal for dropping art, music and physical education from the fourteen-to-sixteen curriculum. There have been other indications that, to meet all sorts of immediate difficulties, the whole concept is to be watered down, and again, in an arbitrary, top-down manner.

There was, of course, originally (I refer to the

proposals in the notorious Red Book of July 1987) a great deal of justified scepticism about this whole initiative, and, given the terms in which it was there presented, this is understandable. But we must remember that the concept of a common curriculum for all – or set of structured experiences covering the main fields of knowledge and culture – was a major objective of the whole comprehensive reform movement of the 1960s and 1970s (and earlier). This movement was primarily concerned to obviate early differentiation between groups of children and their consequent segregation, so in effect shutting off access to fuller life opportunities for considerable proportions of the nation's youth. I well recall the early endeavours (back in the 1950s) to show that a common curriculum within the comprehensive school was a practicable possibility. That was the stage when it was necessary to combat the official ideology that children with different types of mind required basically different forms of education – the great majority being destined for secondary modern schools conceived as schools for working class children 'whose future employment', as an official Ministry pamphlet put it, 'will not demand any measure of technical skill or knowledge' (*The Nation's Schools*, 1945).

That is why, in the present circumstances, the tendency must be to seize on what is positive, or can be made to be positive, in recent legislation. And why one may have sympathy with Peter Newsam's assessment which, while severely critical of some aspects of this legislation, includes the claim that the National Curriculum entitles all children to 'a common set of education experiences pitched at a high level'. Sir Peter is reported as believing that the establishment of this entitlement is the most important achievement of the 1980s.[1]

Now, whatever our criticisms of the thinking, or lack of thinking, behind our National Curriculum – of the assessment procedures now being developed, of those for 'consultation' relating to programmes of study, of the Working Parties and all the rest, I believe we should accept Peter Newsam's evaluation of the overall significance of this move. I will not attempt an historical assessment as to why it is that a National Curriculum, so defined, was actually written into the Act, nor of the major criticism that it is not in fact 'national' since the Secretary of State's own children and those of the governing elements in our society are specifically exempt. This would take us too far from our immediate concerns. But some credit, at least, must be given to the whole lengthy struggle of teachers and others, against continuous government obduracy, both Labour and Tory, for the single exam at sixteen. This movement was fuelled with the same concept as that of the early comprehensive pioneers. Whatever their faults and weaknesses, the sections of the 1988 Act relating to the curriculum can be interpreted partly as a culmination of what was, essentially, a healthy movement having the educational interests of the mass of the children at heart.

If we accept this analysis, what follows? The results are bound to be contradictory – but this is the nature of all educational development within a divided society and one which, as recent research by Dr Halsey and others clearly indicates, is becoming increasingly polarised. On the one hand, let's assume that, over time, this entitlement curriculum is in fact provided for all – a big assumption in the circumstances. That would involve a great gain. Let us assume also that the four key stage assessment proposals are also put in place, though here there is certainly room for controversy and battles. If these follow the pattern proposed by the Task Group for Assessment and Testing (TGAT), as seems likely, what will be the outcome? The entire school population will emerge from the eleven years of compulsory schooling distributed among each of the ten levels. This distribution, I am advised, is bound to follow the pattern of our old friend the normal or Gauss curve; the majority will be bunched around the mean (say levels, 4, 5 and 6 or 5, 6 and 7) – diminishing numbers will be on levels 8, 9 and 10 at the upper end, and 3, 2 and even 1 at the other end. In the words of the now famous anonymous high DES official in his interview with Stewart Ranson, each will have been educated 'to know their place'.[2]

But will they? Here we can foresee a fundamental contradiction – one which lays hidden motives bare. Do we, or the powers that be, genuinely want to educate everyone to the highest possible level? Or do we want them to be educated 'to know their place' in an increasingly divided and hierarchical society? Here Lawrence, who was seized of this contradiction, had something very significant to say.

The idea is alive, he argued in his 1982 Goldsmith lecture, 'of criticism grounded in knowledge provided by the school and of literacy as a gate which lets people into the means of thinking for themselves and becoming critical of our society'.[3] But, he asked, is this entry into critical thinking to be the privilege of an educational oligarchy? Is it being stifled in the state system?

The English system, he said,

> is notable for being in the power of those who do not commit their own children to it and it is accordingly

vulnerable. The powerful still do not favour the cultivation among the lower orders of the scepticism and critical intelligence that is valued among their betters. It is for that reason that they point backwards to basics in the face of the potential of the exciting curricula in literacy and numeracy and knowledge to be found in the recent curriculum movement, in the leading state schools and in the more enlightened private schools.

He went on to argue that,

The decline in investment and support for public education in this country at the moment [1982] is at many points a vindictive, rather than a prudent, economy. At stake is more than 100 years of adventure beyond the mere basics, a span in which schools have – fitfully no doubt – tried to make people independent thinkers capable of participation in the democratic process and of deciding what the future of their society shall be like. Perhaps a faith in expansion and progress underlay that provision for the citizen. We must now find ways of ensuring that a defensive, and more apprehensive, establishment in the context of a contracting economy does not make a critical education an education reserved for privilege.

These words were not lightly spoken. They form the concluding paragraph of what was, I believe, Lawrence's last public pronouncement in March 1982 – just eight years ago. They therefore deserve to be taken extremely seriously. Nor were these words, and this judgement, mere rhodomontade or rhetoric. On the contrary, this judgement arose out of Lawrence's own final research project, looking, as he put it, at academic sixth forms and the growth of independent study. He found the private schools well equipped, with plenty of money, able to re-form their libraries, to buy more books, to provide everything required for high level study on these lines. At the worst end of the state system, on the other hand, he found sixth form students saying that there are not enough books to go round the class, and that those books the school does possess are torn and coverless. This, then, was what he called 'the binary divide'. 'There is a real division,' he said, 'and I think the division is widening.' But there was, he felt, a deeper reason than mere economy for the conditions he found in the people's schools – the fear of critical thinking, of the potential uses of literacy. It was this fear – of the power of independent thinking – which was the most important factor underlying the parsimony affecting public education. This, he described, as a 'vindictive, rather than a prudent, economy'.[4]

It follows, surely, that at this clearly crucial moment of change we need to seize with both hands the opportunities that history has, perhaps unexpectedly, given us. The National Curriculum is there on the statute book for whatever reasons. Can we transform it into the 'common set of educational experiences pitched at a high level' which Peter Newsam sees as 'the most important achievement of the 1980s'? And in the process of transforming it along these lines, can we not also aim to introduce those modifications which will change it from a top-down, managerially inspired and bureaucratic initiative into a flexible instrument which, while providing the necessary structure to ensure progression, leaves scope for, indeed encourages, local, school, even teacher variation according to the strength and specific characteristics of different traditions, schools and teachers? Such, I suggest, must be the perspective.

And if it is a statutorily based entitlement

curriculum, imposed by Act of Parliament, then government has a very clear and specific responsibility to ensure that the legal requirements they have laid down are in fact implemented. Historically, governments in this country have established by Act of Parliament standards relating to school buildings, to safety measures, to school meals, travel and many other matters – for instance defining the years of compulsory schooling. Now, for whatever reasons, the government has taken it upon itself to define the curriculum in state schools (or most of them) involving the definition of attainment targets, programmes of study and assessment procedures. It remains now the clear responsibility of government to ensure the implementation of these measures in all the schools of the country, both primary and secondary; to provide effectively for the supply of the required number of qualified teachers in each of the defined subjects or subject areas; to ensure the provision of the necessary resources, in terms of books and equipment, for all schools and pupils, since without all these the programmes of study and the National Curriculum generally cannot be effectively implemented. As we all know, these are huge tasks, but in fact only part of what needs doing. No previous government in the history of this country has ever undertaken so enormous a responsibility in the field of education. It is surely our job to ensure that the extent of this responsibility, voluntarily undertaken by this government, is fully understood – by the people at large and by the government itself; even if, as Lawrence said in the closing words of his Goldsmith lecture, 'a defensive and more apprehensive establishment' may even now be seeking to ensure that a critical (which requires a full) education is one reserved for privilege. That option must be closed. In drawing attention recently to the extreme backwardness of this country in education, Sir Claus Moser has, I believe, rendered a public service of great value. Perhaps this will help trigger a national movement for fundamental change in which the full implementation of the National Curriculum, modified through discussion and experience, must form a part.

I want at this stage to make a clear and definite assertion. It is that, if we genuinely wish to offer a full entitlement curriculum, or set of common educational experiences, to *all*, this requires, at least at the current historical stage, the full and deliberate implementation of the principle of comprehensive education – and in every area of the country (there are still wide areas, for instance in Kent, Lincolnshire and elsewhere, where the divided system still holds out, though popular local campaigns are now developing in some of these areas demanding an end to this anomaly). Lawrence himself was highly critical of the previous set-up. In his inaugural lecture on appointment to his chair at UEA in 1979, he wrote:

> Historically the great majority of the children of this country have been offered in the state educational system, whether through the elementary school or the secondary modern school, no more than a rudimentary education in the basic skills and such an acquaintance with knowledge as might be expected to inculcate a respect for those who are knowledgeable.[5]

Elsewhere, a little earlier, Lawrence made the point that now that the transition to comprehensive secondary education was secure, full attention could and should be turned to the curriculum – since the structural base for the provision of an effective secondary education for all had been achieved. But here, perhaps, there was a certain over-optimism. Can one doubt that, today, the full development of comprehensive education, on the brink of achievement, one might say, in the 1970s, is under threat; that the reinforcement of hierarchic structures within and now also outside local authority systems is in danger of creating a situation which negates the positive aim of provision of the crucial common educational experiences for all?

There are many aspects of the Education Act of 1988 which have this tendency, intended or unintended. LMS, open entry, encouragement of increasingly sharp competition among schools for pupils – the whole competitive ethos being deliberately developed will, if full rein is given and taken, inevitably result in winners and losers – and in the losing schools there will be tens and even hundreds of thousands of pupils (and teachers) who will lose out. That is one threat, or set of threats, but there are others.

The most important of these relate to local government, its status and role. My own earlier analysis of both Bill and Act interpreted it as predominantly an attack on local government, and especially on its historic role in the provision of local systems of both primary and secondary education, and of course also further and higher education. This is too big a question to go into here, but recent events have made it clear to all, surely, that the conflict between central and local government, particularly on financial issues, is increasingly sharp, while from the 'think tanks' of the right increasingly shrill demands are heard proposing the removal of education altogether from local democratic control. Within education – and those areas that

most directly concern us – the deliberate downgrading of the responsibilities of local government is
expressed through two specific initiatives, both
relating to the construction of Margaret Thatcher's
third tier of schooling: grant maintained schools and
city technology colleges (CTCs). Both directly
threaten the stability of local authority 'systems',
and, by destabilising these, both directly act to
destabilise local comprehensive systems. In this
sense, then, we cannot now accept that the
comprehensive reform – *the condition* for effective
curriculum renewal having a universalistic character – is secure.

Both these initiatives are being pursued with a
certain steely purpose. Four separate units have
been established within, or close to, the DES to
propagate or administer these developments – the
head of one of them was knighted recently 'for
services to education'. By such means signals are
given as to where the real priorities lie. It is well
known that the intention is to persuade the great
majority of schools to opt out, and there is now talk
of further legislation to expedite this move.

But, if we make a realistic assessment of the
situation, it is difficult not to reach the conclusion
that both these initiatives have run into difficulties.
By April 1990 only some 32 schools had been given
the go-ahead for grant maintained status (although
this total had risen to 44 by August of that year) but
the great bulk of these were escaping reorganisation, amalgamation or closure resulting from local
authorities' perfectly legitimate, indeed necessary
attempts to rationalise provision in a period of
demographic decline. Schools originally expected to
head the rush to opt out – successful comprehensive
schools in affluent areas – are conspicuous by their

absence, as are schools in the areas of what the media and others described as the 'loony left'. In fact what has emerged, and clearly, is an overall loyalty to local authorities and (dare I say it) to the values these embody, together with a determination to retain local school systems intact and under local democratic control. Of course we cannot know what the future will bring, and, as has been made very clear, the financial inducements now being offered, especially in terms of capital allocations (but also recurrent), are out of all proportion to those offered to the mass of the schools remaining within local authority systems. How far this condition can be allowed to continue is, in my view, highly debatable.

My conclusion is that the competitive, go it alone ethos, is far from emerging as dominant. The traditions of mutual assistance, co-operation, involving decisions determined by the good of all rather than some – traditions built up in over 100 years of local administration of education – appear to be too powerful to collapse at a single blow. There is, then, hope for the future, but, to use Tawney's phrase, it will be as well to keep our pistols primed and our powder dry.

The Secretary of State has recently given the go-ahead for three more CTCs – in Wandsworth, Telford and Derby – after a novel (in this instance) exercise in 'consultation' in which, it has been reported, the great bulk of the responses expressed total opposition to these initiatives largely on the grounds that their establishment would damagingly threaten local authority systems – that is, local neighbourhood comprehensive schools. We have seen 'consultation' of this kind before – relating to the original Bill. One wonders what is achieved by this method of spurning those immediately concerned with such contempt – unless it is to underline publicly just where power lies, through its naked exercise. But it is worth noting, as relevant to my argument, that this initiative also has, to date, run into the sand – the Treasury, apparently, having called a halt owing to the massive and unforeseen drain on the Exchequer for what are known as Baker's beacons. The limit has been set at twenty, though plans for all these have not yet been finalised. Industry has been sceptical, preferring to siphon what resources it is prepared to make available to the maintained system generally. Some CTCs have already an unsavoury history – in terms of financial and political skulduggery. But now plans are being cooked up here also for a wide development of CTCs through utilisation of the voluntary-aided category. So here also the future is unclear, and for this reason also we need to keep our powder dry.

All such initiatives need close monitoring. This must, of course, be done with an open mind in order to discover just precisely what is happening. Educationists, teachers, local and central government officials, politicians, parents – all have a need to know the precise significance of such initiatives both in their own terms and those of the wider system or set of systems of which they form a part. Recently Tony Edwards, John Fitz and Geoff Whitty published their research evaluation of another such initiative – the Assisted Places Scheme; to my mind a model of achievement in terms of approach and methodology.[6] Research projects on a similar scale are now under way relating to both the GMS and the CTC initiative. The Economic and Social Research Council, and some grant awarding charities, have a certain autonomy, and funds have been made available. This is certainly a positive feature of the current scene. There is, however, a real danger of prostitution of research where funding is provided by the bodies themselves responsible for the initiatives to be studied. But this raises issues which, if very much BERA's concern, lie far outside the scope of this lecture.

To return to the main argument, these initiatives, however justified their rationale (and this could be a matter for debate) are certainly designed to strike a sharp blow at locally controlled systems of comprehensive education. For those who still hold to the ideals that fuelled this movement since the Second World War, 'The over-riding, simple and clear objective of local authorities', in the words of Lancashire's Chief Education Officer, Andrew Collier, 'is to fund excellent educational opportunities for all the nation's children.' Mr Collier made this point at the conclusion of a speech (to the Society of Education Officers of which he is currently president).[7] If I may express my own very carefully considered judgement on both these initiatives, it is that both are politically and educationally irresponsible. Unable to shake comprehensive education by a direct attack, the technique now resorted to is circumvention, and the profference of glittering gifts. *Timeo Danaos et dona ferentes*, as the Trojans rightly assessed a comparable offer long ago. I fear the Greeks even when bringing gifts.

What is the conclusion to all this? It surely must be clear. We need not only still carry through, complete and further develop the comprehensive transformation (especially and urgently into the sixteen-to-nineteen age range), but also buttress and armour it against further depredations. This is a clear condition for realisation of the more ultimate aim – that of ensuring, so far as possible equally for all, a common set of educational experiences, and at a high level. To achieve this the teachers, pupils, all concerned must not be having to look over their shoulders all the time to see where the next threat is coming from – they need stability; they need encouragement; they need resources; and they need confidence in their own ability to transform the situation to reach the desired and, dare I say it, agreed objective. This is the task for the future.

There is another related question that needs discussion. As is well known, Lawrence put his faith, if that is the right word, in what he called inquiry-based teaching – in research as the basis for teaching (the title of his inaugural lecture); in what he called 'action research', where real classrooms are our laboratories, in the charge of teachers, not researchers. 'The teacher who founds his practice of teaching upon research', he said, 'must adopt a research stance to his own practice: it must be provisional and exploratory.'[8] It is this, he argued, that marks him (or her) out as a professional. Earlier he had referred (anonymously) to a very dear mutual friend, sadly no longer with us, Margaret Gracie, known, accordingly to Lawrence, at CARE as 'the hypothesis teacher' – 'a tribute', as he put it, 'to her capacity to stimulate hypothetical thinking within Bruner's social studies curriculum, MAN, a Course of Study.'[9]

The stimulation of hypothetical thinking – teaching as a research-based activity, a process that must be 'provisional' and 'exploratory' – these were Lawrence's objectives, and I think they are objectives that we can all embrace. It is this stance, as I understand it, that characterises the reflective teacher – one who submits his or her own practice to a consistent appraisal. To achieve this is surely no easy task, but if we are to empower our youth – to enable them to achieve rationality, to be articulate, tolerant – in short to develop as students, then the teacher's reflective role, action research, a continuous questioning must be the hallmarks of success. So my question is – how far is this possible, indeed practicable, in the new dispensation now coming into being? In short, will the programmes of study, attainment targets, assessment procedures and all the rest – including the built-in school versus school competitive element, create a situation where the teacher-researcher movement cannot survive? I put it starkly in this sense so that the issue is clear. For many of us, I believe, this movement, concerned as it is not only with classroom processes but also those relating to the functioning of the school as a whole, has represented a nodal point of change – a hope for the future. The professionalisation of teachers in this sense must lie at the heart of the educational process as a whole – pointing the way to better schools, to the improvement of practice, BERA's own objective.

No one outside the schools today can answer this question – least of all me. But this issue needs discussion. It raises complex questions, since each subject presumably presents different problems, relating to the conditions now statutorily being laid down relating to each, while what the position now is for those teaching cross-disciplinary areas certainly also needs attention.

May I now, finally, attempt to draw the threads together and in so doing to formulate what might be acceptable as a broadly-based platform of advance – as guide line for the future?

First, then, should we not attempt to secure, or at least to move steadily and clearly towards, a concept, or transformation of the National Curriculum along the following lines:

Firstly, that it should become a truly *National* Curriculum relevant to and applying to everyone, of whatever school, public or private. No rationale has been offered favouring the exemptions now applying, and deliberately written in from the start. I refer here to the so-called independent schools and the CTCs. A National Curriculum should and must be truly national.

Secondly, that the National Curriculum should be transformed to allow greater flexibility – and in particular scope both for innovation (or curriculum development) on the part of teachers, schools, local authorities, if within agreed, democratically determined guide lines. That it should also allow variation in relation to the needs, and specific characteristics, of particular areas, schools and even individuals or groups of teachers working in similar areas.

Thirdly, that the National Curriculum should be conceived in Peter Newsam's terms, as a set of common experiences, and that working groups of teachers and others should be established to identify these experiences, not necessarily tying themselves to the crude subject differentiation now being established.

Much could, and perhaps should, be said here about assessment and its role. I am not, however, the person to venture into this minefield so only draw attention to this lacuna which others are far better qualified to fill.

I have made three points about the National Curriculum, but my second major point concerns organisation. We need, I suggest, actively to support local authorities, not only in defence of their existing school systems, but, more important, in their development. For nothing can or will stand still.

Further, local authorities need support in developing their systems as truly comprehensive, providing as far as possible, as Andrew Collier put it, 'excellent educational opportunities for all the nation's children'. This policy certainly requires the use of positive discrimination to compensate for built-in disadvantages, particularly in heavily populated areas. Also schools must be encouraged not so much to compete with each other – even if there may be a place for emulation – as to co-operate together, and of course with parents and local populations, to ensure the best possible provision. A culture of internecine strife can hardly be good for education (as was very clearly recognised by the public schools in the late 1930s when a similar situation exploded there due to financial stringency).[10] The second point, then, is the need to ensure stability through support for the development of local comprehensive primary and secondary school systems, now under attack. Success here is a necessity if the first objective, relating to the curriculum, the quality of teaching and learning, is to be achieved.

And third – as a condition of development, of the improvement of the schools and education generally, the extension of the teacher-researcher movement – a new empowerment through the involvement of teachers generally, having the objective of extending the influence of this movement which Lawrence saw as the key to the ultimate improvement of the educational process generally. It is of course the teachers who carry through the real work of education. They cannot accept the role of 'agents' for the 'delivery' of the curriculum, in Keith Joseph's memorable words. On the contrary, they can and should be the government's allies in the desired creative renewal of the work of education – of teaching and learning. So, perhaps prematurely answering my own question of a few moments ago, the answer I would give is yes. Teachers can and must continue to play this role, to develop it more widely. In such involvement lies the true hope for the future.

I close with a single comment about Lawrence made by a local teacher who had been on a CARE part-time MA course:[11]

> I used to so love the quality of his mind: the range, the understanding, the subtlety and delicacy of expression made his thinking very beautiful and his kindness and tolerance made *him* very beautiful.

We cannot all be like him, either in his person or in the depth, the subtlety and sharpness of his thinking. But to renew acquaintance with Lawrence is directly to clarify guidelines for the future. In this sense he is still very closely with us.

Notes and References

1. *Times Educational Supplement*, 29 December 1989.
2. Stewart Ranson, 'Towards a Tertiary Tripartism: New Codes of Social Control and the 17+' in Patricia Broadfoot (ed.), *Selection, Certification and Control*, London 1984, p. 241.
3. Lawrence Stenhouse, 'Curriculum and the Quality of Schooling', in Leslie A. Smith (ed.), *Curriculum and the Teacher*, London 1982, pp. 10-11.
4. Ibid.
5. Jean Rudduck and David Hopkins, *Research as a Basis for Teaching, Readings from the Work of Lawrence Stenhouse*, London 1985, p. 123.
6. Tony Edwards, John Fitz and Geoff Whitty, *The State and Private Education: An Evaluation of the Assisted Places Scheme*, London 1989.
7. *Education*, 26 January 1990.
8. Rudduck and Hopkins, *op. cit.*, p. 126.
9. Ibid., p. 121.

10. See Ron Wallace, 'The Act and Local Authorities', in Michael Flude and Merril Hammer (eds.), *The Education Reform Act 1988, Its Origins and Implications*, London 1990, pp. 235-6.
11. University of East Anglia, School of Education, *Newsletter* No. 1, n.d. 1982/3. This publication includes many personal memories of Lawrence Stenhouse, mostly by local teachers.

5 What Future For Education?*

Fifty years ago, in March 1940, at one of the largest congresses ever organised by the National Union of Students, a resolution was passed by a huge majority urging

> the building of more schools, the opening of the public schools to all classes, reorganisation of the school curricula to include proper physical, sexual and vocational education ... improved free school meals, close co-operation between teachers and parents ... equal opportunities in education for rich and poor alike [and finally] a total reorganisation of the Board of Education [now DES] and of the systems of training and remuneration of teachers.[1]

I start with this since I was there. Not a bad programme, it might be thought, looking back over the decades. So, even in those days there was pressure for change – for increased investment in education, for improved conditions for both teachers and pupils, for equal opportunity across the board. Only recently Sir Claus Moser has called for a Royal Commission on education having rather similar objectives, though of course up-dated and modernised.[2] Today, half a century later, our schools and

* Delivered as a paper in September 1990.

system generally face many more problems, and of a different order, than they did in 1939 or 1940. As regards the call for a Royal Commission, in spite of their bad odour in recent times, we should remember that such enquiries have not always been ineffective. Historically these have been the chosen instruments to effect change in English (and Welsh and for that matter, also Scottish) education. The Cross Commission, as one of its side-effects, prepared the way for serious university involvement in public education for the first time in modern days – this, in itself, can be assessed as an historic step. But twenty years before that, we had the great series of mid-Victorian Royal Commissions which certainly had a profound effect on restructuring and forming the modern system of education, with all its faults (or some would say strengths). Starting with the two commissions on Oxford and Cambridge in the early 1850s (one for each, of course), there followed the Clarendon Commission (on the public schools), the Taunton Commission (on endowed schools), and of course the Newcastle Commission (on elementary schools): later there followed the Samuelson Commission (on technical education), the Cross Commission (again on elementary education) and finally, in the 1890s, the Bryce Commission, which laid the basis for England's very belated system of publicly provided secondary education. These commissions, and particularly the first three (or four), I have argued elsewhere,[3] constituted a crucial 'moment of change' in English education, even if they laid the basis for and hardened up the structure of an hierarchical system, comprising five levels, or sub-systems, each tailored to cater for and indeed enhance the social class divisions in an increasingly polarised society. Recent research of high scholarly quality has shown, first, that the Schools Inquiry Commission represented the victory of the aristocratic-gentry element in mid-Victorian society, and certainly not that of the rising middle class – I refer to David Allsobrooke's thesis in his fascinating study *Schools for the Shires*. It has also shown beyond any question that the Clarendon Commission on the public schools was, in fact, a front for a whole series of highly questionable measures directed specifically at salvaging (and actually privatising) Eton, then and now the leading school for the governing class or groups of this country, from going down under the weight of outraged criticism at the malpractices then existing – I refer here to Colin Shrosbree's outstandingly interesting and thorough recent publication entitled *Public Schools and Private Education* – specifically an analysis of the Clarendon Commission and subsequent legislation.[4] So we can now say that the actual outcome of these commissions was not all positive. But what is impressive in the work of these commissions is their intensive, systematic character. The Schools Inquiry Commission, for instance, published its accumulated data in 22 large volumes – every one of the then existing 800 or more endowed grammar schools was visited and reported on, often by assistant commissioners of high calibre, for instance, T. H. Green, later the Oxford philosopher; James Fraser, later a distinguished Bishop of Manchester, and others. They set to their work with considerable vigour, and carried it through intensively – looking at the needs of society as they interpreted these over the coming decades. Although we may now be critical of the outcomes, we might note that they were not so much seeking immediate answers to currently pressing problems as long-term solutions to crucial social and educational issues. That, perhaps, is why their work, in all cases followed by legislation, has endured so long. When he called for a Royal Commission, I suspect it was this aspect of their work that Moser had in mind.

In this century we have had only one educational enquiry similar in scale to the great – or classic – Victorian commissions. That, of course, was the enquiry into higher education carried through, also with considerable energy and at a high speed, by the Robbins Committee in the early 1960s. This was not a Royal Commission (the idea was mooted at the time, but rejected – by the universities I believe – as involving procedures that might prove too radical). The Robbins Committee was in fact appointed by the First Lord of the Treasury (who happens to be the Prime Minister), and is unique in that sense. But in all other respects it operated like a Royal Commission. It had powers to obtain evidence, and much was forthcoming. It was served by a brilliant group of statisticians of whom Claus Moser was head. It also published many volumes of evidence and statistical data. Finally, in its report, it set out a detailed strategy covering the development of higher education over a period of twenty or more years, and comprehending within its brief all forms of higher education then existing.[5] It is interesting to remember that it was not, in fact, asked to report on a strategy for expansion (which is what it did), but to consider 'the pattern' of higher education and make recommendations on this (which it did also). As so often happens, the circumstances of the time determined the committee's activities and the thrust of its report. The Robbins Committee in fact provided practical guidelines for the future, and, though of course there have been variations, it is remarkable to what degree that future was actually predicted in the report, even though governments (of both hues) combined to reject the Robbins vision of a unitary system and, incidentally, their proposals relating to full university involvement in teacher education. Both these decisions may be regarded as in line with over 100 years of pusillanimous decisions about education which, people are now beginning to recognise, lie behind Britain's present unfavourable comparative position on many indicators in the international league tables. These adverse decisions were not, however, the responsibility of the Robbins Committee. The point I want to make is that Claus Moser, in calling for a Royal Commission, was issuing a call for a thorough, professional, contemporary examination precisely of Britain's relative backwardness in the field of education, now increasingly highlighted, together with the formulation of a series of measures, both short-term and long-term, needed to put things right (no easy task, incidentally, and being rendered more difficult with every year that passes). That is why, I suggest, he called for a Royal Commission. What are needed, in the first place, are effectively laid plans to transform our ailing, elitist and damaged system to meet the challenges of the later 1990s and the twenty-first century.

Claus Moser has done us all a service by articulating so clearly, and in such a challenging way, the real causes for concern with the condition of British education – the 'major deficiencies', as he put it, which are undermining the country's well-being, with 'dire consequences' (his words) for the future. Many children now receive what he defined as 'a totally unacceptable education deal ... not worthy of a civilised nation'. Britain was in danger of becoming 'one of the least adequately educated of all the advanced nations ...'; though there are 'islands of excellence' (Moser cited in particular the Open University), viewed as a whole our system 'has sadly declined and no longer matches Continental Europe, Japan ... or the United States'.[6] This relative decline, he suggested, has deep historical roots.

Today two out of three young people leave school at the earliest opportunity – sixteen; a 'new deal' for those aged sixteen to eighteen was now of vital importance. A levels also require urgent attention while the whole post-sixteen vocational training system (or lack of system) needs overhauling. Moser also questioned acceptance of a 'strikingly privileged' (as he put it) independent sector whose fortunes contrasted vividly with the declining state of local comprehensive schools and the education provided for ethnic minorities. The conditions under which the teaching profession operates also need transformation – it is no longer a prestige profession and this urgently needs changing. Limited access stands out as the most unacceptable feature of higher education. Overall, government expenditure on education has declined from 5.5 to 4.9 per cent of GDP between 1980 and 1987 while present proposals involve yet a further cut in real terms. Neither the government's present educational reforms, nor the Labour Party's alternative, Moser suggested, seek to reverse the present malaise. Neither was attempting to take the required 'leap' in priorities, quality or vision. Decision making is 'piecemeal', and the absence of a coherent framework increases the confusion, and helps to keep standards down.

Moser's appeal was for recognition of the

seriousness of the present situation, and for some form of action which could at least lay the foundations for an all-sided, complex strategy aimed at ensuring a fundamental transformation before it is too late. But it is, I fear, characteristic of our present masters that an immediate, totally negative (and totally doctrinaire) response was accorded to Claus Moser's appeal just a day or so later. 'Michael Fallon, the schools minister, yesterday rejected the idea of a Royal Commission on education, put forward earlier this week by Sir Claus Moser, president of the British Association,' reported the *Independent* on 23 August 1990. 'Every substantial point in Moser's speech', the report continues, 'was dismissed by Mr Fallon' in what was described as 'an uncompromising speech'. What has been lacking from British education, he is reported as saying, is 'the discipline of the market-place', 'the power of the customer', and 'the engine of competition'. With a jibe at those in public life in the 1960s (in my view by far the most productive post-war decade in education to date), Mr Fallon (a founder-member of the No Turning Back group of MPs and of the Adam Smith Institute) concluded by claiming that the national curriculum would generate a rise in educational standards across the board, and that he, Mr Fallon, was 'confident that this country will enter the next century as well educated and equipped in science as any of our competitors'.[7]

So we are instructed, by government representatives, to put our faith in the market and market forces (the engine of competition) to solve our problems, and thereby specifically to reject resource to foresight, analysis, rational planning – the search for optimum means of disposing of what must always be limited resources; bearing in mind the welfare of all as within a democratic society. The crucial issue at stake has been well put by the editor of the *Times Higher Education Supplement*, though here in the context of a discussion about the coming election. Education, he suggests, will be at the centre of controversy over this period:

> At stake is the central element in the government's domestic policies since its 1987 victory. Temporarily eclipsed by the poll tax flare-up, obscured for the moment by the arid complexity of privatisation, education nevertheless is the decisive ground on which two visions of Britain must compete, *private market* and *public good*.[8]

'The Future in Education: Which Way?' was the title I gave the university when asked for it several months ago. This is exactly what I had in mind. We are, it seems to me (and to many others) at a moment of decision. Are we to take the road of the market? Or are we to seek the future of education accepted and valued as a public good – with all that this conception implies – including as an essential precursor a really thorough investigation of the present position, across the board, on a par, at least, with the achievement of the Robbins Committee of the 1960s, and of the great commission investigations of the second half of the nineteenth century?

Now of course such an undertaking would not be necessary, indeed a scandalous waste of resources, if we can in fact rely on 'the market' to sort everything out (though it is perhaps worth pointing out that none of 'our Continental competitors' as Mr Fallon puts it, who are well ahead of us on most of Moser's indicators, have themselves taken this road). But perhaps we can now look briefly at this proposal.

The concept of the market, or rather of its

inevitably beneficent operation, derives, as is well known, from Adam Smith. Indeed a flow of polemical literature pours from the so-called Adam Smith Institute today, as well as from a plethora of others venerating the great Scottish economist – the Institute of Economic Affairs, the Hillgate Group, the No Turning Back Group already mentioned, and all the rest. And all of these espouse and present the market solution. From here derives the call 'Away with LEAs',[9] the call (from Mr Fallon himself) to 'break the local government monopoly' – to free education from the malign hands of locally elected representatives. What we need to do to set everything right, it is argued, is really very simple. Create a market in education. Ensure that the conditions exist where educational institutions (schools, colleges, universities and polytechnics) are forced to compete against each other to survive (and prosper). This achieved, everything will improve. In contradistinction to Gresham's Law (formulated by an earlier economist), the good drives out the bad. The latter go to the wall; but that is the guarantee that the good, who emerge victorious, go ahead with renewed energy. The problem for government is to provide the circumstances where these conditions operate. At the present moment, as far as the schools are concerned, this policy points in a negative direction: destroy, or render powerless, local education authorities, at present responsible for local school systems. The Adam Smith Institute's latest publication, for instance, which it assured me recently contained a 'distillation' of all its thinking on education, is entitled *Schools Out* (you can guess what from).

What, then, was Adam Smith's argument? He proclaimed the 'fundamental beneficence of a "natural" market order'. In so doing he was arguing against contemporary (mid-eighteenth century) mercantilist notions pressing the need for state intervention in the economy. It was the pursuit of individual self-interest, within a free market, which would lead to the mutual benefit of all, and so maximise the public good. The market had multiple advantages. It allowed the greatest degree of individual liberty. It provided incentive to enterprise – a competitive spur to efficiency. And by encouraging the pursuit of individual self-interest, it inadvertently promoted the good of the whole community. By pursuing his self-interest, Smith argued, a man is 'led by an invisible hand to promote an end which was no part of his intention' – that is, the common weal. Therefore it followed: the government should limit its powers. There was, according to Smith, 'a strong presumption against government activity beyond the fundamental duties of protection against foreign foes and the maintenance of justice'.[10]

Now let us assume that this theory, and thinking, can be transplanted crudely, as it were, into the world of modern education – as Mr Fallon and others would have us believe. Let us ask this question: is there a market in education (in Smith's sense), and indeed, can there be?

Education is not directly similar to other commodities (refrigerators, television sets, avocado pears) which are bought and sold on the market. It is a process of interaction between human beings that takes years and years. It is, therefore, highly labour-intensive. Average fees at private (boarding) schools – the 'top' schools – have recently been reported at £8,000 a year:[11] five years (thirteen to eighteen at a typical public school) therefore now costs £40,000 – a considerable sum (and remember the outcome cannot always be guaranteed and you cannot have your money back).

What proportion of the population can afford to buy in this market? I don't know the answer, but we do know that, at present, about 7 per cent of the child population attends independent schools. Of course, not all are as pricey as those I've mentioned. Day schools are cheaper, but even here, I'm advised, the cost is in the region of £3,500 a year. So to that extent, the market is broadened beyond those attending the top schools. And incidentally, we should remember, the commodity on offer is not necessarily priced as it should be in a genuinely 'free' market. State-determined conditions such as charity status, full financial support for a substantial number of pupils (children of diplomats and the armed services), measures like the Assisted Places Scheme (very thoroughly investigated by Professor Edwards and his team recently)[12] – all these distort the market in favour of certain specific 'customers'.[13]

So, in spite of substantial state subsidies (which should not be morally acceptable to proponents of Adam Smith's 'free' market), the goods available are at present restricted to, or only available to, about 7 per cent of the population (at any one time).

We could conclude that this, then, is a funny kind of market. But we could ask, how can access to this market, with all its imperfections, be widened? How can more people be brought into it so that it can begin to operate as the government (or its representatives) apparently intend?

Realistically there is only one way. Only if the state (which theoretically, according to market proponents, should not intervene) hands out the wherewithal (that is, the cash) to huge tranches of the population, so that not merely 7 per cent, but 50 per cent – even ideally 100 per cent of the population (with children of school age) can buy that commodity (education) in the market – remembering that, as provided by private or 'charity' concerns at the moment, this will cost at least £3,500 a year for each child.

But, as a matter of fact, the actual average cost per pupil/student in England and Wales in 1986-87 (the last year for which figures are available) was just over £1,500.[14] The unit (pupil/student) is a composite of both categories – for school pupils alone it would be lower. It will be noted that the sum the state expends per pupil/student is a great deal less than what the top boarding schools charge; but also well under half of what the average run of independent schools charge. But this is another story.

What would be the cost to the taxpayer (and poll-tax payer) if this road were taken (that is, state intervention in the form of handouts to all children)?

It is, of course, impossible to say; but, clearly, it would be roughly the same as the present cost of running the school system, a cost which at present falls on the taxpayers – that is, if the system were run at the present level of facilities and conditions. There might, of course, be marginal savings in favour of either method (for instance, in administrative costs), but it would be impossible at this stage to evaluate them.

The conclusion is quite simple. The state *must* subsidise education – or anyway the great bulk of it. It is simply too expensive – far too expensive – for individuals or their parents to pay for it themselves without the help of society as a whole, which accepts education as a public good, even though a few of the more fortunate members of society can do so and do so now. This is perhaps more a comment on existing inequality of incomes (or wealth) than anything else. However that may be, either the state (and local authorities, if they are permitted to continue in being) provide this education, as is the case now in this and every other advanced country, or (theoretically) the state provides free access to education by handing the cash direct to the consumers (or rather, their parents) in the form of vouchers, credits, or whatever.

If the latter course is pursued, this hardly creates a 'market' in the ordinary, accepted, sense of the term. It is a highly artificial creation – it is certainly not a 'natural' market in Smith's sense.

That is why the *Financial Times*, which surely ought to know, describes it as a 'pseudo-market' – the term 'pseudo' signifying, according to the OED, 'in composition, sham, false, spurious', or as 'deceptively resembling' something. Thus a pseudo-market is not a market, but something which deceptively resembles one. But whatever the meaning that can be attached to this term, both solutions are predicated on a large exercise of initiative *by the State*.

May we consider for a moment the relative advantages of a system powered by consumer choice within a pseudo-market of that kind, and of a system provided by the state and local (or other public) authorities by which education is embodied, as it were, as a public good?

Consumer-led systems in education, it seems to me, are likely to arrange themselves in hierarchies, and to lead to the reintroduction of selective processes, however covert. Some of the more 'popular' schools, will be the most sought after. By contrast, at the other end of the scale, are the least popular, or rejected schools. These, their pupils and teachers, will suffer. Finally they will be closed. Competition between schools – internecine strife – will benefit some but bankrupt others. A sort of anarchy of development will be substituted for system. Overall planning for the future, according to agreed criteria, cannot take place. Whose job would it be to undertake this function? The likely overall outcome will be a complex of schools adapted to carry through the function, as analysed by the French sociologist Bourdieu, of ensuring precise reproduction of existing social and class (and probably also ethnic, religious and even gender) distinctions. The school, to quote the title of one of Bourdieu's more famous articles, 'as a conservative force'.[15] So much for the vaunted 'radicalism' of this solution. Indeed if the vouchers, credits or whatever which are handed out may be topped up with private money, as advocated by many of those supporting this move, this result would be achieved even more quickly, since the incentives leading to inter-school differentiation now become even more powerful. By this means schools would become differentiated more precisely according to the income levels and other features of the local population. In short, state intervention, through the imposition of such a system and the creation of just such a pseudo-market, would inevitably lead to even sharper differentiation and polarisation of school provision than exists at present. Indeed this is surely the hidden or covert objective of this policy. The real issue for this country now, however, it might be thought, is not how to *increase* this differentiation, but how to *reduce* it.

There are many other aspects of the consumer-led,

competitive principle which should be discussed, but shortage of space compels us to leave the argument there. Can we now turn to consider education in its character as a public good?

In this case, the underlying objective of policy becomes, or could (and should) become, the provision of a service tailored to maximise the educational and personal development of all the pupils – and I repeat *all*. As Andrew Collier, Lancashire's CEO and president of the Society of Education Officers put it recently, after criticising very sharply the city technology colleges initiative, 'the over-riding, simple and clear objective of local authorities (and it is these which, under our present dispensation, actually provide the schools), 'is to fund excellent educational opportunities for *all* the nation's children'.[16]

There can and must, of course, be discussion, controversy, even hard fought battles, as to how this objective can best be achieved; but this is open to public participation and decision at both a national and local level. Such discussion and decision can and should take on board all the issues which Moser raised as crucial to our future: comprehensive education, the 16-19 age group, access to higher education, the place and standing of the teaching profession, and so on and so on. It seems ridiculous even to have to argue this point; but the fact is that this represents an entirely different road to that proposed by Mr Fallon and others – that of putting our faith, and our future, in the 'hidden hand' of market forces, in consumer power and the so-called 'engine of competition'. The editor of the *Times Higher Education Supplement* is right: we are now at the cross-roads of decision.

Can we return now to the classical economists

from whom this new view derives legitimacy, or so it is claimed, and especially to Adam Smith, the proclaimed guru of the market educationalists?

That this is so turns out to be unfortunate.

Why?

Certainly Adam Smith argued strongly for the beneficence of the market, as uniting all interests through the 'hidden hand'. But those who call on Smith as their saint and authority in the financing of education have either not read him for themselves (which I suspect is very likely), or have failed to realise that Smith made certain exceptions in his advocacy of the primacy of the market. These exceptions included of course, defence (as we have already seen) but also ... you've guessed it ... *education*!

Nor was this only because he was a Scotsman who believed in education, having drunk in that doctrine from John Knox with his mother's milk, as it were. Not at all.

Smith's impassioned argument for what amounted to state involvement (in the circumstances of that time) in the provision of education for all – and the poor especially – and his specific rejection of the market solution as inadequate, was based on a closely reasoned argument, set out in some detail in Book V of the *Wealth of Nations*.

The argument, which is (or should be) well known, was based on the adverse effects of the fine division of labour which advanced forms of manufacture were bringing in and which, he saw, was bound to develop. Concentration on 'a few simple operations', he observed, makes the labourer 'as stupid and ignorant as it is possible for a human creature to become'. Such employment dulls men's minds, brutalises them, renders them incapable of rational thought – above all, incapable of recognising the need to act effectively in the defence of their country. In these conditions a healthy citizenship requires, necessitates, education. This also will render the people more tractable. The more the people are instructed, he wrote,

> The less liable they are to the delusions of enthusiasm and superstition, which, among ignorant nations, frequently occasion the most dreadful disorders ... They are the more disposed to examine, and more capable of seeing through the interested complaints of faction and sedition, and they are, upon that account, less apt to be misled into any wanton and unnecessary opposition to the measures of government.[17]

Education, then, was a paramount matter of concern by the state; though it is noteworthy that it was then seen primarily as a means of social control – of ensuring preservation of the existing social order. Nevertheless, in these terms, it was now valued by Smith as a public good. Smith himself rejected the market solution, as I have already mentioned, even though he did feel that competition kept people on their toes. He believed, for instance, that Glasgow University's system, whereby professors received their fees directly from the students attending their courses, was preferable to the Oxford system where these emoluments were secured through endowments. As regards schools, however, Smith proposed that these should be established in every parish or district, as in the case of the Scottish parish schools. These should be financed by what amounted to a rating system, but imposed by statute throughout the country (as they were then in Scotland).[18] Smith, then, was certainly not a believer in leaving educational development to the market – to consumer interests alone. On the contrary, the *main drive of his argument was directed towards winning conviction for state intervention.*

Nor was Smith the only one among the classical economists who took this line – at a time when it was not particularly popular, at least among the governing classes. Malthus, a few years later (in the early nineteenth century) did the same, and with even more passion. Convinced, as he was, that the salvation of the poor lay in their own hands, their miserable condition being due to their tendency to propagate excessively, he argued strongly that this truth should be diffused among the people for their own good, and to divert their evident (and then growing) wrath against the governments of the day which they saw as the immediate cause of their suffering. So Malthus also very strongly advocated the provision, through action by the state, of a system of parish schools where he proposed that in addition to the subjects suggested by Adam Smith, the poor could be taught the Malthusian principle of population and the virtues of restraint.[19] Malthus strongly supported Whitbread's Bill of 1807 – the first to propose compulsory education in England and Wales, involving the creation of parish schools financed, again, by local rates.[20] The Bill failed, but Malthus must certainly be numbered among the strongest supporters of state (though local) provision of education as a 'public good' – as interpreted in terms of the circumstances of that time. Once again the immediate objective is social control – preservation of the existing social order in a period of potentially revolutionary upsurge. It was not until later in the century that, as J. K. Galbraith put it recently, it became an 'accepted truth', though now 'partly forgotten', 'that public education is the first step to economic progress'.[21] However, we should remember that in the early nineteenth century Ricardo also, to complete the circle of classical economists, actively assisted in establishing schools for the poor – his wife ran a school for 130 children at their country seat in Gloucestershire.[22] James Mill, McCulloch – indeed the whole army of economists now burgeoning at the outset of the industrial age – were all believers in state involvement. These clearly saw education as a public good, in the provision of which both state and local authorities had a central role to play.[23]

The arguments of the economists and their allies, at a crucial phase of Britain's industrial development, never unfortunately proved strong enough to force the issue. And, in a sense, that is the tragedy of British education. Just at the time when our Continental 'competitors' (as appears now to be the received description) were establishing state supported, cohesive 'systems' of primary, secondary, even technical and scientific education up to a high level, and including vocational and apprenticeship provision, we in Britain still continued to rely largely on voluntary initiatives and market forces, lauding 'diversity', and sadly, primarily concerned, as the great Victorian commissions unfortunately showed, with the use of educaton as mediating, and indeed exacerbating, existing differences between the social classes. As the School Inquiry Commission, for instance, put it in 1868, 'education has become more varied and complex ... the different classes of society, the different occupations of life, require different teaching'.[24] Under this dispensation, it could indeed be said that the main function of education then emerging was not so much to

ensure the reproduction of society with a frag-
mented or divided class structure as the actual
reinforcement of an hierarchical society in which
each stratum knew, was educated for, and accepted
its place. Even at this crucial stage, this is what
determined development. 'Educational systems',
writes Geoffrey Best in his study of mid-nineteenth-
century Britain, 'can hardly help mirroring the ideas
about social relationships of the societies that
produce them'. Education became 'a trump card' in
the great class competition. The result he concludes,
was that the schools of Britain 'not only mirrored the
hierarchical social structure … but were made more
and more to magnify its structuring in detail'.[25] So,
in Best's view, education reinforced and indeed
exacerbated class differences. This view is generally
held among historians. Harold Perkin, for instance,
characterises developments in the 1860s as
intended 'to put education in a strait jacket of social
class'.[26]

If this was the prime consideration, as I believe it
was, then it is understandable that the plea of the
economists was forgotten; that state involvement in
the modernisation of education had at first to be
introduced by stealth; that when universal
education was finally introduced, decades after
similar measures in France and Prussia for
instance, it was through an Act involving a weak
compromise with increasingly ineffective voluntary
initiatives; that when a state-supported system of
secondary education was finally, and in comparison
with others very belatedly, constructed (after 1902),
it was done in such a way as to exclude the great
majority of the population who even now are denied
access to an effective system of education and
training. So also Britain fell further and yet further

behind, on all the main indicators, as Andy Green has so graphically shown in his recent book, *Education and State Formation*, subtitled, 'The rise of Education Systems in England, France and the USA' – the first serious, all-embracing, socio-historical, cross-national analysis of this whole phenomenon.[27] In my view this should be required reading for all government ministers, whatever their hue or degree of dampness, since it reveals the historical roots of what has been called 'the British disease' which has landed us at our present level of relative backwardness so vividly, and indignantly highlighted by Claus Moser.

Green concludes his book, referring to recent legislation, on a sombre note. A national curriculum he sees as long overdue, but, he adds, this 'modernising measure', which genuinely breaks with past traditions, 'co-exists in contradiction with other measures ... which are designed to create a "market" education system', that is, a system 'which returns to the *laissez-faire* traditions of the last century'. A voucher system, now demanded by the neo-liberal new right would, he says, 'create a new hierarchy of elite schools' and so greatly increase educational inequality. Opting out, CTCs, financial delegation, open enrolment – all these measures aim to create competition and so expose institutions to market forces. The results of all this, he concludes, on the last page of this lengthy and impressive book

> will not only be to create greater class division in the independent sector but also to undermine remaining public provision, making planning and rationalisation difficult, and undercutting any otherwise beneficial effects from the national curriculum. If the past has any lessons at all, it is that the mechanisms of the market and the ideology of *laissez faire* serve education

very ill indeed. It would be a sad irony [he concludes] if the country which was the last to create a national education system, and which never quite completed the job, should be the first to dismantle it. It remains to be seen whether, in the name of market liberalism, England again becomes the 'worst educated country in Europe'.[28]

It may be thought that I am ending on a sombre note – and indeed I am. And that this is hardly an appropriate way to conclude a celebration of the centenary of this institution. But we are exhorted today to be realistic and this is just what I've attempted. We have to face reality, but my main purpose is to argue that the real choice has now become abundantly clear for all to see. Reliance on market forces to determine the future? Or full acceptance of education as a public good, with all that that involves?

Moser's call, which was met with so immediate (and should one add, thoughtless) a rejection, was a call for the latter solution – for a thorough professional study of all the key issues, elucidation on that basis of a plan of action, and for its implementation. The objective is clear: to transform the situation by conscious action so that, instead of being as he put it correctly, 'one of the least adequately educated of all the advanced nations', we become one of the best – a centre of excellence. We have seen that the legitimacy of the claim that the market solution is founded on the outlook of Adam Smith and other of the classical economists is a nonsense – indeed a fraud. Their view was the opposite.

It is, therefore, good news that the British Association together with other prestigious organisations, is planning to go ahead with the Moser initiative notwithstanding its instant rejection by those in authority. And there is no doubt that public concern about the state of education in this country is growing, and with increasing rapidity; indeed the contradictions now becoming manifest are bound to increase the strength of popular and informed criticism.

It may be, therefore, that we stand now at the edge of a new break-through, parallel, perhaps, to that which this country (and other countries) experienced in the early 1960s – that decade which, although traduced in the present demonology (and specifically in relation to the rejection of Moser's proposal), in practice saw tempestuous advances in education right across the board – in the universities and higher education generally (where it started), within secondary education where what C. P. Snow described at the rigid crystallised structure was at last broken open, and also within the primary schools which, for the first time historically, came in from the cold. Not all was achieved which might have been, as I've already suggested, and in some areas there were, perhaps exaggerations. But that decisive, in the sense of irreversible advances were made, including, incidentally, a new level of funding, is undeniable.[29]

I suggest we may stand at just such a point – poised for a new 'break-through'. This will take effort, and struggle, by all of us; for nothing comes easily or automatically – especially now.

Notes and References

1. *Students in Congress*, Report of the British Student Congress, Leeds 1940, National Union of Students, pp. 32, 15.
2. See *Education*, 24 August 1990; *Independent*, 21 August 1990.
3. In Brian Simon, *The Two Nations and the Educational Structure,*

1780-1870, first published as *Studies in the History of Education, 1780-1870*, London 1960; for a more recent assessment, see Brian Simon, 'Systematisation and Segmentation in Education: The Case of England' in Detlef K. Muller, Fritz Ringer and Brian Simon (eds), *The Rise of the Modern Educational System, Structural Change and Social Reproduction 1870-1920*, Cambridge 1987.

4. David Ian Allsobrooke, *Schools for the Shires, the Reform of Middle-Class Education in Mid-Victorian England*, Manchester 1986; Colin Shrosbree, *Public Schools and Private Education, The Clarendon Commission, 1861-1864, and the Public Schools Acts*, Manchester 1988.

5. *Higher Education. Report of the Committee appointed by the Prime Minister under the chairmanship of Lord Robbins, 1961-1963*, Cmnd 2154, October 1963.

6. Report in *Education*, 25 August 1990.

7. *Independent*, 23 August 1990.

8. *Times Higher Education Supplement*, 7 September 1990.

9. The title of a pamphlet by Sheila Lawlor (1988).

10. Acknowledgement for this succinct summary must be made to Andy Green, *Education and State Formation*, London 1990, p. 252.

11. *Independent*, 5 September 1990.

12. Tony Edwards, John Fitz and Geoff Whitty, *The State and Private Education: An Evaluation of the Assisted Places Scheme*, London 1989.

13. For an authoritative recent assessment of the extent of financial support from the taxpayer to independent schools, Caroline Benn, 'The Public Price of Private Education and Privatisation', *Forum*, Summer 1990.

14. Brian Simon, *Education and the Social Order, 1940-1990*, London 1991, Appendix Table 17.

15. The classic presentation of Bourdieu's standpoint is Pierre Bourdieu and Jean-Claude Passeron, *Reproduction in Education, Society and Culture*, London 1977. See also Pierre Bourdieu, 'The School as a Conservative Force: Scholastic and Cultural Inequalities' in Roger Dale *et al.* (eds), *Schooling and Capitalism*, London 1976, pp. 110-117.

16. *Education*, 26 January 1990.

17. Adam Smith, *An Inquiry into the Nature and Causes of the Wealth of Nations* (1838 edn.), Bk.V, Ch.1, Art, ii, pp. 350-353.

18. Ibid., p. 352.

19. For Malthus's views, Brian Simon, *The Two Nations ...* pp. 142-3 (see also T. R. Malthus, *An Essay on the Principle of Population as it affects the Future Improvement of Society*, 1878 edn., Bk. IV, Ch. 9, pp. 436-441).

20. Patricia Jones, *Population Malthus, His Life and Times*, London 1979, pp. 140-1.

21. *Guardian*, 8 September 1990.

22. P. Sraffa (ed), *The Works of David Ricardo*, Vol.X, p. 169. See also Brian Simon, *The Two Nations ...*, p. 136.

23. Brian Simon, ibid., pp. 138-148.

24. Schools Inquiry Commission (Taunton), *Report*, Vol.1, (1868), p. 93.

25. Geoffrey Best, *Mid-Victorian Britain, 1851-1875*, London 1973, p. 170.

26. Harold Perkin, *The Origins of Modern English Society 1780-1880*, London 1969, p. 302.
27. Andy Green, *Education and State Formation, The Rise of Education Systems in England, France and the USA*, London 1990.
28. Ibid., pp. 315-6.
29. In Brian Simon, *Education and the Social Order, 1940-1990*, four chapters are devoted to developments in higher, secondary and primary education in the 1960s.

6 The Education Reform Act: Causative Factors*

It may be that there is now a breed of 'policy analysts' who could make light of the task of analysing what lay behind Kenneth Baker's 'reform' of education. But I am not one of them. Nor are there any simple answers. Interpretations of the factors lying behind the whole confusing field of contemporary educational change are hardly likely to come up with logically cohesive sets of propositions identifying and outlining the reasons for our present discontents. This would involve reducing highly complex phenomena to simple cause and effect analysis, as required by the typical old fashioned examination question: 'Give the three main causes for the outbreak of the Great War'. Nowadays cut and dried answers demanded by this type of question are of no value whatever. Things are a great deal more complicated than can be fitted neatly into such a package. On the other hand, interpretations by, for instance, neo-pluralist sociologists seem to err too far on the side of complexity. I will attempt, therefore, to steer between these two extremes, and, further, rather than come up with a set of reasons behind current developments, ask a set of questions or raise issues

* Delivered as a paper in July 1991.

which may, I hope, be relevant and at least stimulate thought.

The educational world has suffered and is continuing to suffer a shock of seismic proportions. Martin Shepherd, Waltham Forest's CEO, in a recent article headed 'We Were Taken to the Cleaners by the Government and the Press', writes that he believes we have reached the point of 'catastrophic shift' in thinking about education in this country, 'My judgement now is that I do not expect to see the public education service in this country recover from the damage done by the changes in the late 1980s within my working lifetime.'[1] About the same time as Shepherd's article was published I received a personal letter from a distinguished Chief Education Officer, recently retired but not so long ago president of the Society of Education Officers. This was prompted by Kenneth Clark's announcement in the midst of the poll tax imbroglio that the government now intended to take over all colleges of further education (and sixth form colleges) from the local authorities, funding them directly from the centre. He cannot see the justification for this action, he writes, adding,

> But of course we're not being governed by Tories but by mystics who see the market as the instrument of Divine Providence. It may keep them in comfort but we shall all have to pay the price of the Hayek doctrine if it runs the full course. It will prove to be a threat to political freedom and the social order.[2]

Just at this time I also received a letter from Harry Rée, written just a few weeks before he died. He commented on the fact that I ended my recent book (*Education and the Social Order, 1940-1990*) on an optimistic note

> as, in public I still do – but I'm beginning to have my doubts. The almost certain economic decline will I fear

buttress the moral decline (can we doubt that?). Signs of hope, I agree, are there – especially in the fine teachers who have stayed on, determined to exert themselves heroically on behalf of their students – and there'll always be such. But I fear that the Tory changes of the 80s will have inflicted a permanent blow to our health as a nation.

He added, characteristically, 'Kenneth Baker owes us an abject apology!'[3]

And here is a High Tory in the sense used by the CEO just quoted, David Muffett, chair of the education committee of Hereford and Worcestershire, reflecting on Prince Charles's recent speech. His sentiments 'must have been gall and wormwood to the Education Secretary', he is reported as saying.

What the government has tried to do over the past four years is to try to create what Mao Tse Tung tried to create through the cultural revolution – unnecessary confrontation, unnecessary change and unnecessary destruction.[4]

'Unnecessary confrontation, unnecessary change, unnecessary destruction.' That puts it rather well. How do we interpret so radical a policy, so deliberate a challenge to accepted procedures? From what or where is the political will motivating the series of actions over the past three or four years, *still* apparently escalating? By what 'sleight of hand', as Michael Ignatieff put it recently in the *Observer*, contrasting the flourishing state of the private enterprise book market with the shattered state of public libraries, of book supply to schools, universities and polytechnics, has a party based on the ideology of free enterprise persuaded so many people that it is, at the same time, a party of modernisation and progress?[5]

How, in short, has this situation come about?

There are, of course, what we might call global factors at work. In his latest volume, recently published, entitled *Power, Competition and the State* (Vol.3), Keith Middlemas argues that, from 1945 to 1975, a 'fragile consensus' existed, or was maintained in British society and politics.[6] He interprets the Thatcher years as a reaction to what he calls 'the very grave state failure' of the mid-1970s in the wake of the oil shocks, hyper-inflation and industrial strife. Thatcher, however, by de-regulating credit especially, put British society 'almost beyond the control of the modern state'. What we are seeing now might, then, be interpreted in this theory as a desperate attempt to restore that control. In this, Middlemas himself stresses the importance of 'hierarchy' in interpreting the past: we possess 'a slow-moving, deeply conservative polity, almost Confucian in its concept of hierarchy'. The imposition, by statute, of a national system of assessment covering every individual (for the first time historically), but with exceptions of course, might be seen as one auxiliary means of establishing, refining and legitimising that hierarchy. As one by now infamous anonymous DES official put it to Stewart Ranson, 'People must be educated once more to know their place.'[7]

Certainly the industrial, financial and state fiscal crisis of 1972-73 marked a crucial phase in the introduction of new policies in education (and elsewhere). The fiscal crisis provided the material ground for monetarist policies which, of course, particularly afflicted the social services whose expenditure must be tax-raised. Keith Joseph, perhaps the leading Tory monetarist in the late 1970s, consistently stressed the extent to which such expenditure reduced resources available to the wealth-producing sectors of the economy. Educational expenditure, in this scenario, was increasingly seen as an unwelcome drain on productive investment and activity – as parasitic. So circumstances created a base for a new climate of discourse. This is the context in which new, radical policies were conceived, the soil in which they found fertilisation.

At roughly the same time, education was increasingly perceived as dysfunctional – in terms of its output, a standpoint given legitimacy by Callaghan's 1976 Ruskin speech. And there we had the first critique, and use of the phrase 'educational establishment' – an idea and concept which the press and politicians (including recently the Prince of Wales) have seized upon and will not let go. This is a clever phrase: to attack an 'establishment' is a radical thing to do – or seems so. No holds whatever have been barred, witness the *Daily Telegraph*'s recent scurrilous attack on Lady Plowden, Sir William Taylor, Denis Lawton and others.[8] This 'establishment' is perceived as responsible for the whole sorry state of English and Welsh education, portrayed as an inert, producer-dominated activity run either by self-interested bureaucrats or by way-out mavericks. So a climate was created which was used to legitimate 'radical' measures – such as most of those in ERA. This also was an aspect of the marginalisation of local education authorities and the teachers and their organisations, marking the end of the triangular 'partnership' so celebrated by Lester Smith and others in the 1950s.

The aura of failure was now effectively fastened on the schools by first, a massive, possibly co-ordinated press and media attack (including the BBC). This was supported, or followed up, by an equally massive critique from industry, or parts of it, typical being Sir Arnold Weinstock's famous 1976 statement and article, 'I Blame the Teachers'. By this time education was being singled out as a real cause of Britain's relative economic backwardness. How far, then, I am asking, were the measures taken later facilitated by the image of schooling now apparently being deliberately created – even perhaps in an organised way? Conspiracy theories are not normally taken seriously by historians, but it is perhaps legitimate to ask how this assault was co-ordinated, and by whom?

Whatever weaknesses there may have been within the educational world, the image of almost total failure now being propagated was surely extreme. What actual truth was there in these charges relating to the schools and their failure? How far were they an accurate reflection of what was actually happening? It is undeniable that there was confusion – for instance, about the curriculum. It is also certainly the case that there were many very serious problems facing schools – particularly those in central London (conveniently near media headquarters) and in some other inner city areas. It may be also that there was a degree of complacency. But if we wish to make a general assessment as to the performance of the school system, there are some indicators which need to be taken into account. DES statistics, for instance, show that, between 1973 and 1987 pupils gaining one or more A levels and those gaining five or more O Levels increased from 20.7 to 27.8 per cent – an increase of nearly 40 per cent over fourteen very difficult years. Over the same period those gaining no GCE/CSE passes fell from 21.6 to 10.1 per cent, a decrease again of about 50 per cent.[9] In respect of earlier rates of advance these were quite quick. Government representatives' responses to these data have been to claim that the advance was too slow. But in the circumstances this carried little conviction. The schools in any case were still being forced to operate a categorisation system developed historically to assist and legitimise the tripartite system, as is well known. This system, in essence, passed (or accepted) 30 per cent and failed, or rejected, 70 per cent – the great bulk of the pupils in the schools. Labour and Tory governments totally failed to grasp this nettle over the period under review. Whether GCSE has done this is another (moot) question. But even within this rigid categorisation structure with its outdated objectives the data in fact show a steady advance. And there are other indicators. Opinion polls have shown, historically, quite strong and consistent support for local authority schools, including comprehensive secondary schools, especially where these were introduced in specific areas. A 1967 survey indicated support rose to 73 per cent in areas where comprehensive schools had been established, and 85 per cent where those questioned had children in these schools. Maurice Kogan reports that a survey a few years ago showed 88 per cent of parents content with local authority schools to which their children went. He cites, in a recent article, a similar return in a survey by Martin Hughes of Exeter University. A *Which?* report showed 90 per cent of users of LEA schools and colleges were satisfied.[10] Primary schools also consistently gain warm support from parents. Hearsay or journalistic evidence perhaps is not acceptable, but the *Observer* recently carried a striking article by a teacher in a private school whose message was the unfashionable one that the children recruited from the state schools were far and away better prepared than those from private schools – in spite of the smaller class numbers in the latter?[11]

In the light of such evidence, what reality was there in the criticisms of the local authority schools and systems? This is clearly important, not only because it is this system that is being, as it were, torn up by the roots, but also because the legitimisation of the whole policy rests precisely on the image of schooling that the press, some (but by no means all) industrialists, ideologists (for instance Black Paperites and others) and politicians have created.

Related to this is another factor that has scarcely, as yet, been taken into account, but which bears closely on the charge that the schools were failing the country. Callaghan reiterated the industrialists' complaint that the schools were not turning out people with the needed skills – industrial enterprise was thereby being hobbled. But, perhaps with hindsight, this critique appears naïve. What was actually taking place in the mid-1970s was a fundamental, and sudden, transformation in the youth labour market itself. The school system – indeed the educational system as a whole, is, and always has been, very closely related to the demands of this market, and it is this relationship which, when operating smoothly, has given the whole system equilibrium. A sudden crisis in this relationship has recently emerged. 'In some respects', writes David Ashton, an expert in this area, 'the current crisis in the relationship between the education system and the youth labour market is the most profound yet.'[12] It amounts to a *'fundamental disjunction* in the relationship between the educational system and the traditional forms of training available to young people'. The types of skills required for contemporary industry, 'have undergone a radical transformation', yet the institutional structures we have inherited for the transmission of skills 'are still geared to the requirements of an economy that has long since passed'.

The analysis is complex and can only be briefly summarised here. Essentially, Ashton isolates four main elements which, over the last two decades, have transformed the underlying demand for youth labour and the kinds of skills employers require. Firstly, there has been an acceleration in the pace at which capital in labour-intensive industries has been relocated (out of this country) to low-wage economies. These industries were traditionally major employers of unskilled and semi-skilled youth labour.

Secondly, the last two decades have witnessed an extension of many product markets from national to global markets, resulting in the virtual elimination of firms relying on their control of the domestic market (motorcycles and cars, and so on). This, together with the deliberate policy of the early 1980s of maintaining a high value of the pound (the third factor), decimated exports. In the world 1980-82 recession plant closures reached 20 per cent of manufacturing output, resulting in massive job losses, particularly in manufacturing industry.

Fourthly, and perhaps most importantly – there is the impact of the new technology. The combination of advances in micro-computer technology with improvements in the design of conventional technology created the computer numerically controlled machines. These involve *enormous* improvements in productivity. The result has been a quantum change in the relationship between employment and output with a devastating effect on the numbers of skilled workers required.[13] This latter development was reaching a decisive stage just at the moment when the Thatcher government's de-industrialisation policy of 1981-82 hit the country. What followed was a massive disjunction between the demands of the labour market on the one hand and the structure and character of the school system on the other – the latter still geared to debouch the majority of its pupils into unskilled or semi-skilled jobs at sixteen as, of course, had long been the practice in this country.

These structural changes in industry meant a sudden, massive rise in youth unemployment in particular. Determined to avoid confrontation with labour organisations, firms sought to retain their workforce through energetically operating redundancy agreements, so securing early retirement on a large scale. But the second arm of the policy was to put an almost complete stop on youth recruitment. This strategy enabled employers to effect a big shift in the structure of the labour force in a relatively short period – two or three years. The school-leavers were of course directly hit by heavy youth unemployment (no jobs on offer) suddenly. One result was the summer riots of 1981 – particularly in Liverpool. This led directly to the setting up, almost as a panic measure, of YOP (Youth Opportunities Programme, one year in duration and costing £1 billion), later YTS (Youth Training Service, lasting two years, with the cost doubled) for low-level training – for semi- and un-skilled jobs, both in fact now rapidly disappearing. These were palliatives, but it was objective factors (for instance, technological change) that led to the disjunction in the first place. In the meantime the traditional forms of youth training – apprenticeship – collapsed. In 1965 some 155,000 young people were so placed and trained. In 1985 the figure was only 73,000 – less than half. By 1988 it was down to under 58,000. 'By the end of the 1980s' writes Ashton, 'one of the main institutions on which Britain relied for training for the next generation of workers had virtually collapsed'.[14] Nothing was put in its place.

The 'blame the schools' argument is dismissed, by Ashton, as a palpable nonsense. The effects of technological change could have been foreseen, plans accordingly made to cope, or indeed, to exploit the new opportunities, as other nations have done. Ashton cites Canada, the United States, Japan, France and Germany, *all* of which have successfully adapted their education and training systems to the new situation with its new demands for higher level education and training – all, incidentally, in different ways according to their own experience and historical conditions. Only Britain took no effective action.[15] Indeed, ironically, the situation that emerged was simply used as another weapon with which to belabour the schools. Irresponsibility could hardly have gone further.

Further, this disequilibrium sent shock waves of intangible strength through the whole system. Young people's expectations were profoundly affected. The disjunction so caused created uncertainty as to objectives and procedures, and indeed as to the legitimacy and purpose of the whole exercise, which was bound to have a negative effect on all concerned with education – local authorities, teachers, students, parents, even the DES. It is difficult to estimate the effect of this factor, but I believe it to have been profound, and, of course, not only still to be operating but also to have, as yet, no clear and agreed means of resolution – rather the opposite.

Only 25 per cent of the labour force in this country is today engaged in manufacture. The new technology greatly enhances the productivity of labour, leading some to estimate that this proportion will decline to 10 per cent over the next few decades. The striking change in the character of the labour force over the last 30 or 40 years certainly has, and already has had, enormous implications for education, and any assessment of the disjunction between the structure of education and the nature of the labour market must take this into account. It is estimated that by the end of the century, 70 per cent of jobs in Europe will require 'cerebral' skills, only 30 per cent manual. In 1950 the proportions were reversed. We can see now that the introduction of comprehensive education, by blurring the sharp distinctions of the past, was an 'appropriate' response in that it introduced a necessary flexibility into the system – in terms of its output. But, as we have seen, built-in rigidities continued, and in any case the transition was unplanned, pragmatic – very English, if you like – and so the opportunities were missed, although perhaps this was not the case in Scotland. If they are to be seized in the future a lot of very hard thinking and determination will be needed. Neither is yet in evidence.

Looking back historically we can see that the education/labour market disjunction of the late 1970s and early 1980s had a decisive significance; the sad aspect of this was that, instead of drawing lessons about the changes required to meet the future, the attack was turned directly on the schools. And this in a period of sharpening fiscal crisis – a

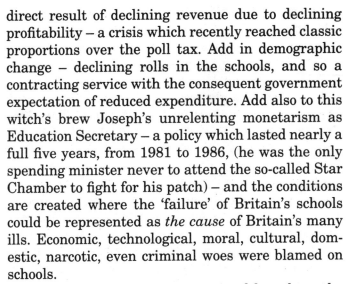

direct result of declining revenue due to declining profitability – a crisis which recently reached classic proportions over the poll tax. Add in demographic change – declining rolls in the schools, and so a contracting service with the consequent government expectation of reduced expenditure. Add also to this witch's brew Joseph's unrelenting monetarism as Education Secretary – a policy which lasted nearly a full five years, from 1981 to 1986, (he was the only spending minister never to attend the so-called Star Chamber to fight for his patch) – and the conditions are created where the 'failure' of Britain's schools could be represented as *the cause* of Britain's many ills. Economic, technological, moral, cultural, domestic, narcotic, even criminal woes were blamed on schools.

The prognosis, I suggest, is false, but the conditions have been created for seismic change. As a matter of historical fact, this was hastened by what were strictly political factors: the effects of the smashing defeat suffered by the governing party in May 1986 both at the municipal polls and at the three parliamentary by-elections rashly held simultaneously at that time. Shortly after, Joseph finally resigned, pushed out, in effect, by his own party. 'We've got to do something about education,' said Margaret Thatcher somewhat belatedly.[16] But the Conservative Party and government still had no clear policy. It was in the vacuum so created that the new right lobby saw its chance. The conditions were propitious. A right-wing Prime Minister was in control. An expert communicator was appointed in Joseph's place. A mass of resources was *suddenly* made available. Here was the moment of change – on the political level.

We may now move to the origins and character of

the new right's offensive, and its product – the Education 'Reform' Act.

It is well known that the groups on the right, which sprouted 'like dragons' teeth', as Andrew Gamble once put it,[17] now saw their opportunity and immediately brought pressure to bear where it was likely to be most effective – on Margaret Thatcher. The No Turning Back Group had already met the Prime Minister a year earlier, when she had asked its members to flesh out their proposals.[18] Their publication, *SOS, Save Our Schools*, proposed independent school boards dominated by parents; direct funding of schools by the DES on the basis of student numbers; the boards having power to fix salaries and determine all expenditure; the right of parents to send their children to any school prepared to accept them – in essence the key measures of ERA. The group was promised that the pamphlet would be required reading for Margaret Thatcher and the Education Secretary during the summer of 1986. These proposals were in fact largely embodied in the Conservative Party's manifesto the following year. The essence of these (and other) proposals – there were many – was to open up the schools to market forces, the ultimate aim being to introduce competition between schools as *the main means* of determining development. To achieve this it was necessary to 'free' the schools from local authority control. They had to be free-standing institutions. The ideological basis of this policy was derived, it was claimed, from Adam Smith, though its authors (and those of several pamphlets published by the Adam Smith Institute) never drew attention to the fact that Smith devotes an entire chapter to his *Wealth of Nations* to arguing that to leave educational development to market forces was, while theoretically desirable, totally impracticable in fact. Here, he argued, was one exception to the beneficent operation of the hidden hand (there were others).[19]

The ideological drive of the new right in education was neatly summarised by Michael Fallon, when he dismissed out of hand Claus Moser's proposal in August 1990 for the establishment of a Royal Commission to investigate and report on an across the board plan for education, to transform Britain's shocking backwardness in this field over the next decades. The rejection was both curt and contemptuous.[20]

To achieve market place conditions several things were perceived as necessary. First, the schools must be freed from dependence on local authorities, in order that they become free-standing institutions and so in a position to compete with each other. Hence the consistent, and some would say unprincipled, attack on these authorities, as well as the unrelenting move towards centralised control – in many fields beside education. The theory, as we know, is that competition will reinforce success and drive out or bankrupt the unsuccessful. What the schools in general do will improve, almost automatically. Above all, it is argued, standards will rise.

We know very little about the policy making process at this crucial phase – that is, in 1986-87 – though Stephen Ball has gathered some relevant material.[21] Perhaps in 30 years' time this may be penetrated at the Public Record Office by future historians, although I suspect that Thatcherite weeders may be at work. But it is surely now clear that the items in the manifesto (revealed in some cases only weeks before the election), and in the subsequent Bill, were not thought up at the last moment and worked out on the back of an envelope as some have held. On the contrary, the package as it appeared in the Bill (and earlier in the Consultation Papers), consisted of a set of carefully thought out and related measures, all aiming at the same end, the power of each depending on the power of all. What was extremely ingenious was the way the movement of opinion in apparently disparate areas, for instance in the field of assessment and the curriculum, was effectively exploited to allow measures to be introduced which related each to all in this very specific package, or set of policies.

This applies particularly to the local management of schools (LMS) and Open Entry sections of the Act, which clearly relate closely together. Both were presaged in certain local initiatives in earlier years (LMS), and in some of the earlier legislation by previous Conservative governments (the 1980 Education Act). These aspects of the Act, together with the elaborate sections concerning grant maintained schools (GMSs) and the single section legitimising public expenditure on city technology colleges (CTCs), clearly directly related to neo-liberal thinking concerning the creation of a market. These structural measures are sometimes differentiated from the statutory imposition of the national curriculum with its accompanying assessment measures. The motivation of this latter set of measures is often attributed to neo-Conservative thinking which stresses centralised state control rather than to the neo-liberalism which focuses on the creation of a market. There may be something in this differentiation. But the really ingenious feature of the Act is that the whole national curriculum initiative is in fact fully integrated, as an essential feature into the overall drive for a market economy which is what the Act is about. It is this which makes the Act a unity and gives it its strength and power.

Why? Because in the search for hierarchy and new means of control, the national curriculum provides, as it were, statutorily articulated tramlines along which all schools must operate. Given this condition, LMS – devolvement of power to parents and/or governors – becomes entirely practicable; any school which operates outside these tramlines faces, in theory at least, the full force of the law. The proceedings around Culloden School recently testify to the power of this theory. So, LMS frees the schools from direct local authority control which, as we know, is the first condition for the creation of a market, but presents no threat to the social order. Open Entry as at present legally defined as ensuring that all schools must accept pupils from areas outside their authority boundaries, means that schools are forced to compete in what is now a wider market for customers. And this, of course, is where assessment fits in according to the theory of the package, since assessment, as first adumbrated very clearly in the original consultation paper or 'Red Book', as it is known,[22] has the function not only of raising standards but also of providing parents with data about the school's 'success', and is therefore seen as the prime means by which parental choices are informed so giving a (spurious) legitimacy to the 'education' market. 'Parents ... should know what a school's assessment and examination results indicate about performance and how *they compare with those of other schools within the LEA or neighbourhood*' (my emphasis, B.S.).[23] The Red Book also states that LEAs must publish annual reports 'showing aggregated examination results over a time series for each age cohort in each authority's schools'.[24] I am not now referring to developments since the whole TGAT (Task Group for Assessment and Testing) operation, as this came later. I am analysing the package as originally presented; and in that original presentation the focus on testing at the ages of seven, eleven, fourteen and sixteen is set very precisely in the context of informing parental choice.

The moves towards a National Curriculum on the one hand and testing (or assessment) on the other, can be seen historically as having different derivations from the structural features of the Act. This aspect must be dealt with briefly. The idea of a common curriculum (the term once widely used) within the comprehensive secondary school was already being widely propagated, by teachers especially, at an early stage in the movement – though no one then even conceivably thought in terms of statutory imposition. As early as 1957 a book by comprehensive school teachers on the importance and the practicability of introducing a common curriculum in all the main subjects was published[25] – the essay on history being contributed by George Rudé, now an elderly and distinguished historian, then a very keen youngish teacher at a well-known London comprehensive. The growing and massive pressure for a single exam at the age of sixteen in the late 1960s was another symptom of this movement. In an open-ended questionnaire Caroline Benn and I sent to a sample of comprehensive schools in the late 1960s no question was responded to with more passion.[26] But the 1970s were in many ways a truly wasted decade and this demand was not successful at the time, in spite of much fruitful work by the Schools Council on its feasibility. Shirley Williams, as minister, prevaricated on this (and most other) issues during her term of office. But the idea of a common curriculum was not a new one in the 1980s. What is of historical interest and significance is the way in which the move towards increasing central initiative and control concerning the curriculum during the 1980s, led by the DES and Keith Joseph, gradually created a situation where action by the government was in principle becoming acceptable, even if the form of the national curriculum as set out in the Red Book came as a sudden and profound shock to the educational world as a whole. However by the summer of 1987 the imposition of a National Curriculum by statute had become politically acceptable – it was a plum ripe to be picked and fitted expertly into the package in preparation. The first official announcement by Baker as to his intention of introducing a national curriculum laid down by statute if re-elected came in his speech to the North of England Conference of January 1987. No mention was made at this stage of assessment, or testing, by this expert politician.

The imposition of a system of national testing (the term is used advisedly) at the ages of seven, eleven, fourteen and sixteen was first raised, I believe, by Rhodes Boyson and Brian Cox in the editorial to Black Paper 4, the new series published in 1975, after the return of the Labour government. The Black Papers, as a phenomenon, must be related historically to that which motivated their origin – the student revolt of the late 1960s. The first such paper was almost entirely devoted to a devastating, or a series of devastating, critiques of the students whose behaviour was regarded not only as insupportable but as presaging disaster for the social order as a whole, to culture generally and to the universities in particular. It was only in subsequent numbers that the Black Paper editors and writers turned their attention on the schools, to focus the critique in particular on what they defined as 'progressive education', on new developments in primary schools and on what they perceived to be the 'failure' of comprehensive schools. Their concern overall throughout this period was the rejection of egalitarianism, support for selective procedures, the restoration of an ethos of discipline, of authority in education, of didacticism in teaching. It was in this context that the testing proposals were made. Their primary concern, it seems to me, was not so much with education as with the social order, which they perceived as threatened by contemporary developments in the schools. This was, of course, not necessarily the government's main motivation in bringing this item into the package. No doubt ministers genuinely felt that the kind of testing (or assessment) they seem to have had in mind would assist in the raising of standards. But certainly they also saw this item as an essential building block in the creation of a market economy. That is its importance. Thus the disparate movements – for a common, or national curriculum on the one hand and for testing on the other – were both ingeniously embodied in the package which was ERA; and the measures resulting related functionally to the structural features of the Act mentioned earlier.

If we can summarise, the objective effect (and ideological drive) of this measure is a turn directly away from the ideals of the past – the provision of 'excellent educational opportunities for all the nation's children', as Andrew Collier has put it,[27] towards the introduction of differentiation, hierarchy, 'variety' and so new divisions within the publicly provided school system – differentiation, variety, being crucial to the concept and the actual working of, the market. So the general direction or thrust of educational provision is transformed, and that certainly is the intention, as has, indeed, been officially announced and confirmed by several responsible ministers, including Messrs Fallon, Dunn and Boyson, not to speak of Kenneth Baker, John MacGregor and now Kenneth Clarke. These have espoused the thinking of organic intellectuals (to use Gramsci's phrase) like Anthony O'Hear who, in his recent pamphlet *Education and Democracy* concludes, 'We need, then, an education system which is divisive, élitist and inegalitarian.'[28]

In the field of education thinking of this kind had been building up since the late 1960s. This was the period when the first publications advocating free market procedures – voucher systems, and the rest – were first propagated. Indeed it is just at the point when the swing to comprehensive education gathered pace and became a popular policy that these ideas emerged and began to make an impact – the first Black Paper was dated 1969. It was also just at this point that the Conservative Party conference saw a determined effort by what was then a minority (but a large one) to break the domination of the Heath-Boyle consensus line on comprehensive education. The further development of this latter movement, which now began to espouse Stenhousian objectives relating to critical thinking, was clearly now beginning to be seen as a threat – perhaps to the haves or even, perhaps, to the social order as a whole. It was now that consensus began to develop on the right if slowly in a sense, rapidly in another, determined to bring this to a halt and to restore hierarchical structures and tighter control in the field of education.

In making an analysis of this kind it is difficult to separate economic, political, ideological and social factors. Over the last two centuries education has been seen by those in authority as mediating the social structure – as a crucial means of enhancing the pre-eminence of the eminent and the deference of the rest. In my view the main motivation for educational change (or lack of it) over the whole period has been that of ensuring, or attempting to ensure, the reproduction of the existing social order as it existed at specific periods. *This has insistently held priority over the alternative policy of modernisation* – adapting to, or attempting to meet the demands of economic, scientific and technological change. I believe the same factors are operating today. The primary concern appears to be to transform the educational system so that once more it presents a bulwark against change and facilitates social reproduction. I am putting it starkly and perhaps provocatively. With Harry Rée I believe that these attempts to turn back the clock to the mid-nineteenth century may well 'inflict a permanent blow to our health as a nation'.

As indicated at the start, I have not attempted a logically cohesive analysis relating crises at one level (for instance, economic) to those at other levels (for instance political or ideological) – partly because interpretations claiming a direct relationship between these areas are now suspect – nor is it clear which, if any, have primacy. The situation is extraordinarily complex; all that seems possible at this stage is to point to some possible causative factors. It is too soon to identify those which have really influenced recent changes with any certainty.

But one thing is clear – that the economic and social structure of British capitalism faced a deep crisis in the mid to late 1970s and later. Both these structures, and governments trying to cope with them, were in disarray.

Education, as a crucial social activity and enterprise, inevitably suffered from these circumstances. The failure to re-adapt and re-structure in the light of powerful objective forces created a highly vulnerable situation. The tragedy is that this was seen as an opportunity to inflict yet further blows, when what was urgently needed was a quick understanding, a true and penetrating analysis of the new situation, and rapid and cooperative efforts by all concerned at all levels to adapt and even transform the situation to extract maximum advantage.

That option was neither taken nor even explored. No doubt it is naïve to suppose that the political process could ever work that way. But actually it has done so in the past – consider, for instance, the new situation of the late 1950s and early 1960s in higher education, responded to by Robbins – with its 20 plus year projections. If it was possible then, why not now? Admittedly circumstances differ, the task is even broader and more all embracing. Time is running out. What, then, are the prospects for the future?

Notes and References

1. Martin Shepherd, 'Where Did We Go Wrong?', *Education*, 10 May 1991.
2. Jackson Hall, letter to the author, 19 May 1991.
3. Harry Rée, letter to the author, 8 April 1991.
4. *Education*, 26 April 1991.
5. Michael Ignatieff, 'Gradgrind Rules in the Public Libraries', *Observer*, 2 June 1991.
6. Keith Middlemas, *Power, Competition and the State*, Volume 3, *The End of the Post-war Era: Britain Since 1974*, London 1991.

7. Stewart Ranson, 'Towards a Tertiary Tripartism: New Codes of Social Control and the 17-plus' in Patricia Broadfoot (ed.), *Selection, Certification and Control*, London 1984, p. 241.
8. John Clare, 'Classroom Trendsetters', *Daily Telegraph*, 24 April 1991.
9. See Brian Simon, *Education and the Social Order, 1940-1990*, London 1991, Table 13, p. 596.
10. Maurice Kogan, 'Education: Problems and Constraints for the Next Government', *Political Quarterly*, Vol.62, No.2, April-June 1991, p. 227.
11. Article by Julia Marlowe, *Observer*, 26 May 1991.
12. David N. Ashton, 'The Youth Training Crisis' in P. Brown and H. Lauder (eds.), *Education for Economic Survival* (forthcoming). For an acute analysis of the whole situation, David Ashton, Malcolm Maguire and Mark Spilsbury, *Restructuring the Labour Market: the Implications for Youth*, London 1990.
13. Ibid., 'The Youth Training Crisis'.
14. Ibid.
15. Ibid.
16. *Times Educational Supplement*, 16 May 1986.
17. Andrew Gamble, *Marxism Today*, November 1979.
18. Brian Simon, op. cit., p. 528.
19. See pp. 109-11.
20. *Independent*, 23 August 1990. See also p. 100.
21. Stephen J. Ball, *Politics and Policy Making in Education: Explorations in Policy Sociology*, London 1990.
22. DES, *The National Curriculum 5-16, a consultation document*, July 1987.
23. Ibid., p. 14.
24. Ibid., p. 20.
25. Brian Simon (ed.), *New Trends in English Education*, London 1957.
26. Caroline Benn and Brian Simon, *Half-Way There, Report on the British Comprehensive School Reform*, 2nd ed., London 1972, pp. 268-9.
27. Andrew Collier, *Education*, 26 January 1990.
28. Anthony O'Hear, *Education and Democracy, Against the Educational Establishment*, London 1991, p. 38.

7 Three Years On*

As mentioned in chapter 1, it was Peter Wilby, then education editor of the *Independent*, who predicted on election day in June 1987 that 'The return of a Conservative government ... will mean the break-up of the state education system which has existed since 1944.'[1] Whether this prophecy proves true or not, I suggested in *Bending the Rules*, depends on the outcome of the struggles over the Baker 'Reform' Bill, 'but that this is the clear intention cannot be in doubt'.[2] This book, hurriedly written in November 1987, was in fact dedicated 'to the memory of those who fought, over the last century, for a full and effective system of public education, now at risk'.

It is a matter of historical fact that a Conservative government was returned, with a large parliamentary majority, at this election. Two major legislative measures were laid before parliament, hailed by Margaret Thatcher as the 'flagships' of the new government: the 'Great Education Reform Bill' (as it was originally called), and the poll tax. Both were carried successfully through parliament in 1987-88, being hardly amended in any significant respect in the process, each supported in the Commons by the 100-plus majority held by the government, and in the Lords – on the crucial issues – by the massive and unscrupulous use of normally

* Written during Summer 1991.

non-attending hereditary peers drummed up for the occasion. It was, perhaps, hardly a glorious victory in either case.

The history of the poll tax is too well known to repeat here. There is no doubt whatever that this initiative proved in practice to be an abject political failure, now abandoned. It will certainly take years to clear up the mess and in the mean time local government has probably suffered permanent damage.[3] The second 'flagship', however, sails on regardless, although the fleet has lost its admiral and the captain command of his vessel. But it was this measure specifically that Thatcher claimed as crucial to the continued hegemony of the Conservative Party (see p. 16). In the eyes of its chief progenitor, then, the Education Act was primarily a *political* measure, designed to create new constituencies of support specifically for the Conservative Party, and so to ensure their continuance in government. To achieve this, within the limits of the resources that might be made available, it was perceived as necessary not only to shock, but more fundamentally to shift the whole basic structure and ethos of education, transforming it from a public service directed at providing (however defined) equally for all, to one powered by market forces having the objective of enhancing differentiation, and so competition, between schools at all levels. For enhancement of the common good was to be substituted the battle of each against all, both in terms of institutions and individuals. Such was the intention – and the appeal – of the new dispensation.

Now, three years after the passage of the Act (and four years after the publication of the initial 'consultation' papers), it is possible to make some assessment of what has been achieved. Has the Act in fact led to the break-up of the system brought into being in 1944? Or is it on the way to doing so? Alternatively, how far has resistance to its provisions been successful in preserving the main features of the earlier system? It is clear enough that, after three years, many of those closely involved are now beginning to think, with Harry Rée, Martin Shepherd and now many others (see pp. 120-1) that permanent damage is being inflicted on the public system of education. Is this assessment correct? And if so, what scope is there to reverse the engines? These are the crucial issues.

As argued in the previous chapter, the Act is, in essence, all of a piece. That is to say, the curriculum and assessment measures fit neatly into an overall package which opens the whole field to the play of market forces, ensures central (state) control at all key points, downgrades the role (and relative autonomy) of local authorities to that of agents, reduces the role of teachers also to that of agents (as Keith Joseph defined them), and, finally, appears to enhance the role of parents both as managers (school governors) and as consumers (through extending parental choice). The measures directed to achieving these objectives are both structural (local management, open entry, opting out, etc.), and related to the educational process within that structure (national curriculum, assessment). We will look first at the structural changes, then at those related to 'process', and finally attempt to bring both together in an overall evaluation.

Local Management and Open Entry

The two most important measures, in terms of the

development of a market – or, perhaps more accurately, of a complex set of micro-markets – are the establishment of local management of schools (hereafter LMS), and Open Entry. The deliberate development of a 'third tier' (in Thatcher's terms) through grant maintained schools (GMSs) and city technology colleges (CTCs) is clearly also seen as a means of enhancing the 'variety' of the commodity on offer, a necessary characteristic of any market. These initiatives will be discussed later. LMS and Open Entry, however, are now beginning to affect the great majority of schools, primary and secondary. Their impact is likely to be the most powerful of all the measures in the Act in bringing about overall change in the direction desired by the government.

There can be no doubt that LMS, in one form or another, is here to stay. It can reasonably be assessed as, in itself, a *potentially* positive measure. But this is where the ingenuity in the construction of the Act as a whole becomes apparent. Devolution of financial management to the schools in itself is desirable, and on the whole welcomed by the schools themselves. The sting in the tail is the link made between this measure on the one hand (with formula funding based on pupil numbers), and open entry on the other. By this link a step perhaps desirable in itself is transformed into a powerful weapon imposing what could become cut-throat competition between schools for survival.

We may first tackle LMS itself – the crucial link with Open Entry will be approached later. Although under the Act this system does not have finally to be brought in until April 1994 (Circular 7/88), by the summer of 1991 it was already very widely implemented. All schemes, designed by local education authorities, involving precise definition of the actual funding formula to be imposed, have had to be submitted for approval, or otherwise, to the DES. The majority of local authorities have already passed this stage and, where these have been approved, schemes are now being implemented. A few authorities have had their schemes rejected, and these are being revised and re-submitted. There is, of course, some scope for variation in these schemes, but this is strictly limited since the Secretary of State (DES) has laid down that the formula must be based primarily on two factors: the actual number of pupils in the schools, and a scheme for age-weighting these pupils (essentially ensuring differential funding according to the ages of the pupils). This is why this system of funding (and management) is described as 'pupil-driven' or 'numbers-driven' rather than 'issue-driven' – that is, determined on strictly educational criteria. 'Financial viability', it is held, 'substitutes for educational viability.'[4]

The money allotted to a school through this, or any other formula, clearly determines, generally speaking, the number of teachers the school can afford to employ. Expenditure on teachers' salaries inevitably swallows up the great bulk of the financial resources made available. An important issue here is the government's insistence that a school's expenditure on teachers' salaries must be calculated on *average* salaries rather than 'historic' or 'actual' salaries (the salaries actually paid to teachers at specific schools). Some schools may have had a larger proportion of senior teachers than others. If historic salaries were paid, the outlay would differ among schools otherwise similar. This condition, of course, also puts an end to a policy of positive discrimination whereby schools in disadvantaged areas are more generously treated than others as a matter of deliberate policy (although provision for children with special educational needs may be built in to the formulae). Insistence on average salaries means that well staffed schools with more than their share of senior (or well paid) teachers will have to shed some of these, and recruit younger and so cheaper teachers. The evident harshness of this measure has been softened by allowing a four-year phasing-in process.

There are two issues here that need clarification. First, originally up to 75 per cent of what is called the Aggregated Schools Budget (ASB) of the local authority had to be delegated to schools. In April 1991 this was raised to a minimum of 80 per cent, the change to take effect in 1993.[5] Up to 10 per cent of ASB, falling to 7 per cent after three years (1993) may be retained by the authority for central services (provision of advisers, school psychological service, etc.). Michael Fallon, junior minister, increased the pressure on local authorities substantially in April 1991, when he announced that the proportion of the so-called 'Potential Schools Budget' to be delegated to schools must rise to at least 85 per cent by April 1993.[6] At the same time Fallon also announced that 80 per cent of the amount delegated to schools must, by April 1993, be determined by the number of pupils in the school. In making this announcement, which clearly acts both to enhance the numbers-driven nature of the system, and further to weaken local education authorities financially, Fallon added:

> Taken together these reforms add up to a significant increase in independence for LEA schools. For many of them I see that as a very major step on the road to total independence, to taking on grant-maintained status.[7]

By such statements the hitherto hidden agenda is made overt.

If salaries of teachers take up the bulk of the school's revenue under formula funding, the residue is available to cover other areas of expenditure, for instance capitation (books, paper, equipment, especially scientific and technological), heating, lighting and other so-called 'day-to-day premises costs'. This is the main area where governors' decisions may now be made – without reference to the local authority. Of course, staffing issues, especially those of a marginal character, are also now matters for governors' decisions relating to overall expenditure.

Local authorities have had some degree of discretion in determining this formula, for instance in deciding the relative weighting allotted to different age bands, building in additional weightings for pupils with special needs and giving additional support to small schools.[8] It is worth noting that formulae submitted and agreed include, in most cases, extra funding for statemented pupils. But no formula covers extra funding for all children with special needs (approximately 20 per cent of the school population), and it is widely held by those concerned with this area that these children will lose out.[9] Another important point worth noting here is that the formulae submitted by local authorities and accepted by the DES *all* reflect the historically determined differentiation of funding by age. Put crudely, a seven-year-old earns a great deal less money for a school than a seventeen-year-old (typically the latter is allotted more than twice as much). In theory a local authority could have proposed equal funding throughout the age range, but no one had the temerity. There is now, however, certainly developing (among primary schools in particular) a demand for more equal funding by age.

This is the sort of issue that is likely to emerge with greater force in the future.

Another issue LMS is bringing into the open is the fact, well known but never precisely quantified, that the cost of a unit (one child), age-weighted, varies by local authority. This variation may be due to two factors which can reinforce each other – first, expenditure per child by some local authorities is a great deal less than that of others, and vice versa; second, these differences may be enhanced by different age-weighting policies. The fact that some very large differences exist between local authorities is now being brought into the open much more clearly than has ever been the case in the past, and this, also, has implications for future policy.

Early experience of LMS appears to indicate that, contrary to expectations, administration of LMS makes few demands on head and senior staff (though contrary evidence is also available).[10] This is because the great bulk of the money goes in salaries. Administration of the relatively small amounts left available apparently presents no great difficulties, perhaps particularly in small primary schools – large secondary schools with sixth forms clearly have greater residual sums at their disposal. Recently, however, the extent to which LMS constrains the staffing requirements of the National Curriculum has become increasingly evident, especially in secondary schools.[11]

LMS, of course, relieves local authorities of much detailed administrative and managerial responsibilities, putting the onus directly on the schools, now responsible for their own budgets. The percentage of the total schools budget (ASB) delegated, as we have seen, has been increased from 75 to 80 per cent. Local education authorities, as viable financial entities, are, therefore, being progressively and relentlessly squeezed, implying a severe reduction in the resources available for funding local authority services to schools, historically developed over many decades. Michael Fallon has recently spelt out the remaining functions which he sees as relevant. These include responsibility for school attendance, the provision of pupil statements (for children with severe learning difficulties), auditing and inspection of schools, and planning and the provision of capital spending. Announcing this perspective, Fallon declared 'once again' that 'Councils will no longer run schools – schools will run themselves.'[12] There could be no clearer statement of the government's intention not only to cut local government responsibilities down to size, but to render them almost powerless (indeed, as we shall see later, their inspectorial function is now at risk). Such actions and statements are directly in line with the government's declared hostility to local education authorities, (and so to local, democratic control over school systems).

Devolvement of budgetary control to individual schools may have positive tendencies, though it remains to be seen whether in fact boards of governors (and heads) administer the (limited) resources available more efficiently than local authorities, whose responsibilities are now being superceded; and whether the teacher time and energy involved in these new managerial activities detract seriously from what many would regard as the more important educational activities of senior staff.[13] Further, through LMS, the burden of actually imposing cuts in educational spending is cleverly devolved on to school governors, as Lord Taylor has recently emphasised (see p. 194). But, as indicated earlier, these policies assume their full significance when operating in their inter-relations. The rationale of the policy as a whole is the creation of a market; competition between schools for pupils, and so for resources, is seen as the engine that will drive the system as a whole. To make a reality of this market, to enhance the power of the consumer, the Education Act included a set of sections designed to enhance the reality of parental choice. These involved negating hitherto existing powers of local authorities to limit recruitment to specific schools, a power used to protect the viability of systems of schools covering specific areas, especially needed in a period of falling rolls. School closures, of course, took place, and with official encouragement from the DES and the Audit Commission, but in a planned and ordered way. By the use of these powers individual schools could be protected from the vagaries of fashion, of sudden variations in recruitment, while the development of the system as a whole could be subject to rational planning in the interests of all, but particularly of the children attending the schools (present and future).

The government's open enrolment proposals, as first defined in the original consultation paper and later embodied in the Bill and Act, were greeted with outright hostility and indeed devastating criticism from almost all those organisations and bodies responding – teachers, local authorities, parents, the Churches, school governors and trade unions.[14] In so far as the proposals appeared to substitute anarchy for rational, democratically controlled planning, they seemed to most respondents a recipe for chaos. There were many also who perceived, under the populist rhetoric, a covert design to enhance class advantage, since it was already clear that the exercise of choice was differentially exercised by social class. Indeed the possession of a car, and time to drive it, clearly greatly extends the capacity to exercise such choice.

It is too early to make any kind of effective assessment of the impact of the link-up between LMS and Open Entry but, implicitly, this provides what is, perhaps, the most powerful weapon yet devised to bring about a fundamental transformation in the ethos, culture and practice of the school system. LMS is still only beginning to be implemented. The first serious impact of Open Entry on school budgets (reflecting recruitment variation) will only be felt from April 1992. From that date, however, the effect is likely to build up over the next few years and perhaps even after that. If this legislation remains unmodified, the close monitoring of developments in this whole area will be essential.

The tendencies that are likely to show themselves can be predicted with some certainty – partly because, through the 1980 Education Act, the scope for parental choice was already widened as a crucial aspect of Conservative education policy. Research has shown beyond any doubt that it is the middle and professional classes which largely predominate in the exercise of parental choice – first, of course, in the decision to send their children to private schools, and, in the case of those who have decided to send their children to maintained schools, in the decision to send them to a specific school of their choice, rather than to the locally provided school, primary or secondary, serving the neighbourhood in which they live.[15] This general pattern was found to be the case in the most complete and serious study carried through to date – 'Parental Choice in Scotland'.[16]

Legislation providing open enrolment was carried for Scotland in 1982, several years before similar legislation in England. The Scottish research study mentioned above monitored the effect of this measure. It reached three main conclusions. Firstly, that the exercise of choice was a function of the opportunity to choose, irrespective of family background. That is, it depended primarily on a number of schools being available in a practical, geographical sense. Secondly, that choice was exercised more commonly by families of 'high social class ... and of high parental education'; that is, it was functionally related to social class. Finally, the study found that the schools so chosen within the state sector tended to be reasonably long established, academically respectable schools, with 'above-average attainment' and pupils coming from above average families in terms of their social and economic status.[17]

Summarising its evidence, the Scottish research team sees parental choice as a policy intended to engineer social change, 'to create a growing class of persons loyal to market principles and the new Conservatism'. 'Fascinatingly,' the authors continue,

> the new inequality [being brought about by these measures] was shaped in the social and spatial mould of an older inequality that comprehensive reorganisation in the 1960s and 1970s had tried with some success to reduce.

This implies that these measures, by circumventing, or distorting comprehensive education, are recreating, in a new mode, the inequalities and divisions of the past. The authors conclude their paper by saying that their findings

> confirm the fundamental sociological tenet that voluntary individual behaviour [in this case the exercise of parental choice, B.S.] is socially structured in ways that reproduce persistent inequalities between groups.

They also suggest that 'The structures through which individuals reproduce social inequalities have been maintained at certain crucial junctures by political intervention.'[18]

This research study appears to bear out widely held predictions that the operation of parental choice through open entry will result in a growing differentiation between schools within the maintained sector. The most 'popular' schools, as perceived by parents, will expand; conversely, the least popular will contract. Such changes will immediately be reflected in the schools' budgets, especially since the authority's proportion of available moneys siphoned to the schools is now put at 85 per cent, while 80 per cent of ASB must be distributed on the basis of pupil numbers. So the 'popular' school expands, takes on new staff, offers yet more to their pupils, while conversely, *and as a direct result*, the unpopular school will be forced to cut expenditure in every way possible, and in particular to shed staff. A downward spiral gets under way which is probably self-accelerating, the conclusion being slow death and actual closure. This latter solution, of course, reduces 'choice' for local parents. Further, the experience of the children in such schools, and of the teachers, is scarcely likely to be life-enhancing.

Over-capacity necessary to system to work

Recently there has been a flurry in the quality (and educational) press on the whole issue of parental choice, and how things are actually working out in the new dispensation. It is now widely claimed that, whatever the rhetoric, parental 'choice' is largely a con, that all a parent can do is to express a *preference*. For such preferences to be actualised requires that there must be space to accommodate extra pupils in all schools so 'preferred'. But where the schools are full, there can be no such scope. The CEO for Harrow, for instance, making this point, is severely critical of the 'choice' rhetoric. His postbag is heavy, he says, with complaints. People think they have a choice, but this is not so in Harrow. There the popular schools are crammed, leaving no room for manoeuvre. 'I have to explain', he writes, 'why there is absolutely no choice of schools available to anybody.' Howard Fielding concludes his article with a sense of exasperation:

> I think I can say quite easily that the people of Harrow, who are to have greater choice extended to them, are already exercising it strongly in favour of the present arrangements. Will someone please give them the choice to stay with the present system and to opt out of the proposed reforms, or is that too much choice to ask for?[19]

In a leader entitled 'Choice is a Slippery Thing', the *Times Educational Supplement* also points up some of the contradictions in this policy. Formula funding has ensured that recurrent expenditure moves with the children, 'But the open enrolment legislation is carefully framed to avoid the capital costs real choice would entail.'[20] This legislation lays down that schools must accept pupils up to the limit of their accommodation (or 'standard number' as defined in the 1980 Education Act). It does not provide for capital funding for extensions. For this reason the full negative effects of open entry are unlikely to appear, although heavy pressure for entry to a particular school will encourage 'creeping selectivity'. Indeed the whole policy certainly encourages differentiation, and that is its significance in the context of this discussion. In the mean time it is worth noting that parental frustration, probably mainly among the middle strata, appears to be mounting. 'We attribute the rise in schools' choice appeals to the current hype that encourages parents to believe that they have a choice,' a representative for the Advisory Centre for Education (ACE, an education consumers' organisation), said recently. 'This is simply not so. They do not have a choice, they have a preference – that is all.'[21] In July 1991 both the *Guardian* and the *Independent* carried full-page spreads on this whole issue, reflecting and reporting on parental frustrations. 'Education Reforms Dramatically Reduced the Power of Some Parents to Choose Their Children's Schools' was the heading of the *Guardian* article by Francis Beckett. 'Every Parent's Right to Choose – and Lose' was that of the *Independent* piece by Karen Gold. 'Any School as Long as it's not Full', was the heading of a second article in the *Independent*.[22] It seems clear that all is not well on the 'parental choice' front. A better policy might be to focus on providing 'excellent schools for all', as proposed by Andrew Collier, and other local authority representatives.

It is the government's intention to enhance market-type conditions in education by the construction, and application, of what are called 'performance indicators', by which it is hoped to penetrate into and analyse a school's performance and express the results numerically, so that consumers (that is, parents), shopping around for the 'best' commodity on offer (that is, education), can be assisted to reach their various conclusions and make their choices.

The only measure so far seriously proposed, however, relates to the publication of the outcomes of 'assessment' at the key stages 1 to 4 (at the ages of seven, eleven, fourteen and sixteen), though the relation between such 'assessment' at sixteen and GCSE results are still unclear. These results, as they become available, must statutorily be published at eleven, fourteen and sixteen, though publication of the key stage 1 (age seven) results, whilst strongly advocated by the government, remains voluntary. The purpose of such publication, and to whom data is to be made available and in what form, was clearly stated in the original consultation paper on the National Curriculum (see pp. 135-6).

One difficulty with such an 'indicator' is that the results will be heavily contaminated (if that is the right word) with social class considerations. It has long been known that children from the upper, more affluent social classes achieve better at school than those of lower; these differentials have been analysed in detail in very many government reports (and elsewhere) over the last 40 years, when sociologists first began making analyses of this kind.[23] That is why it is widely understood that, if it is necessary to make a comparative analysis of the gains children achieve by attending a given, specific school compared with others, the 'raw scores' derived from examinations or assessment need to be modified to take into account this social class factor. Hence the impassioned debate that has been going on as to whether assessment data, when published, is to be so modified. Unsurprisingly, the government (or Secretary of State) has clearly stated that it is the raw scores which should be published, on the grounds that these are what parents want to know. The objective result of this practice will, of course, be to ensure that at the head of the columns (or league tables – a term now being widely used), will be schools attended by a higher than average number of middle or professional class children. Publication of data in this way will clearly act as a powerful factor ensuring differentiation between schools through the exercise of parental 'choice' in any locality.

The matter is, in fact, a great deal more complicated than this. As McPherson has pointed out, teaching is only *one* of the factors affecting children's learning, and so achievement (examinable or otherwise). Research in Scotland has identified at least ten separate factors which affect children's attainment, quite apart from the contribution of school management and teaching, all of which should ideally be taken into account in any assessment of a school's performance. These include the prior attainment/ability of the pupil when he or she first arrived at the school, his or her socio-economic status, the average ability of the other pupils at the school, the level of deprivation in the home neighbourhood, the level of local unemployment and other factors.[24] Whether any or all of these will be taken into account in assessing whether a school has met agreed objectives (or in compiling 'league tables') is exceptionally unlikely. Certainly, without more expert assistance than is now available, parents cannot be provided with this information. Most choices, then, will be made in the dark.

Opting Out: Grant Maintained Schools

We have dealt, so far, with LMS and Open Entry, as
instruments for the enforcement of market conditions on the schools. These affect *all* maintained
schools, both primary and secondary, and it is this
which gives these measures their power. But the
Education Act, as is well known, also laid the
statutory basis for the establishment of two new
types of school, grant maintained schools and city
technology colleges. Both were to provide free
education, but neither was to form part of local
education authority 'systems'. Indeed, to achieve
grant maintained status, a school (or its governors
and/or parents) had deliberately to opt out from local
authority control. These two types of school,
although different in character, were to form
Margaret Thatcher's 'third tier', comprising what
she initially defined as 'state independent schools'
funded directly (in large part, at least) by the state.
Part of the rationale provided by government
representatives for these initiatives was the need to
provide 'variety', so widening consumers' choice, and
in effect assisting to give education some of the
characteristics of a genuine 'market'. Another
argument follows the same line of thought, or
ideology – that by their example, and through their
competition, these will act directly to raise standards across the system as a whole.

Both these initiatives have been referred to in
earlier chapters. The intention here is to up-date
that material and assess the overall position as it
had developed by the summer of 1991. This is
increasingly difficult. The political need for quick
successes spurs new initiatives, at almost breakneck
speed. This has proved particularly to be the case in

relation to opting out – the establishment of grant maintained schools as a new category. We may first assess these developments and go on to consider their implications for the future, and the health, of the system as a whole.

It is worth recalling at this stage that the original consultation paper on grant maintained schools specifically stated that 'grant-maintained schools *will compete on equal terms with the local authority sector, and will be funded on the same basis as other schools in their neighbourhood*' (my emphasis, B.S.). This principle, according to Fitz and Halpin (in their research paper on this issue) 'has been restated by successive ministers who have also taken some care to explain that schools should not seek to opt out because they see a financial advantage in doing so'.[25] The rationale, apparently, was 'to demonstrate that grant maintained schools, once outside their LEAs, could manage the same amount of money more effectively, and thus be more responsive to their "customers" '.

If this was the original policy, and it appears it was the case, it was not long before it was overturned. Opting out did not, at first, appear to be a popular policy, as we have already seen. Ballots were few and far between; applications came in slowly, and, in the majority of cases, these were from schools threatened with closure or reorganisation. Very few schools appeared to want to 'liberate' themselves from local authority control and financing, and this in spite of an energetic, and expensive, campaign launched by the semi-official, industry-dominated and financed unit set up to propagate and lead this move, and in spite of the clear and publicly expressed wish by Margaret Thatcher as Prime Minister that the great majority of schools

should and would take this step. But political
reputations were at stake. The removal of the
majority of schools from local authority control and
influence was now clearly a major political objective,
particularly since, by this means, local authorities
could be cut down to size in what is by far their
largest responsibility. In that sense, this policy
chimed in with what was increasingly clearly the
government's   overall   policy   *vis-à-vis*   local
authorities.

The announcement of the first capital grants to
grant maintained schools in January 1990 certainly
put into question the government's rhetoric relating
to equal funding. The second such grants a year
later further reinforced this scepticism. Those to
GMS schools averaged about £300,000 per school in
the second year; in the previous year they had
averaged £276,000 compared to £15,000 for all other
schools. No wonder the journal *Education* asserted
that this route is now 'blatantly paved with gold'.[26]
There could be no doubt whatever, in the light of the
enormous disparities now shown, that the offer of
substantial financial inducements to opt out was
now deliberate government policy, although this
was consistently denied by the responsible ministers
and indeed denounced as 'paranoid nonsense' by
Kenneth Clarke.[27] In October 1990, at the Conservative Party conference, John MacGregor already
announced four new measures designed both to
facilitate opting out and to ensure that those taking
this step would be substantially rewarded financially. Firstly, the size limit was lifted, so enabling
all primary schools to take this step (originally there
was a size limit of 300 pupils); secondly, the
so-called 'transition grant' given to all schools
accorded grant maintained status to help them over

the move was doubled; thirdly, the 'specific grant' again given to all schools was increased; and fourthly, the formula capital allocation was also increased. MacGregor also announced that a law *compelling* all schools to ballot on opting out was under consideration. As Fitz and Halpin point out, these measures, taken together, 'can be interpreted as undermining two of the principles embedded in the original policy: financial neutrality and the power of parents to determine the timing of the change of status'.[28]

Only a month after making these announcements (November 1990), when under mounting criticism from the Tory right for not pursuing a sufficiently aggressive policy in education, John MacGregor was displaced as Secretary of State by Kenneth Clark in a Cabinet reshuffle. The latter has made abundantly clear, in many public statements, that he fully supports the move to opt out and that he also expects the majority of schools to take this step – further that he (and his junior ministers) see no future for local authority control, or even involvement in education (though no alternative has yet been offered). Clarke's own clear personal involvement was epitomised by his triumphal visit to Bourn primary school in Lincolnshire, the first primary school to opt out, bearing the news of their success, complete, of course, with photo opportunity; as also his later personal visit to the Arnewood School, the hundredth opted-out school.[29] It seems now to be very clear that, if the Conservatives win the next general election, measures will be taken to ensure that the great majority of schools do, in fact, take this road. If this happens, then Peter Wilby's prophecy, cited at the start of this chapter, will be shown to have been accurate.

What, then, is the current position in this area? Local Schools Information (LSI) closely monitors the situation. Its April 1991 information indicates that all secondary schools (about 4,250) and about 3,300 primary schools have been eligible to opt out since the Act became effective on 29 July 1988. About 17,500 primary schools with fewer than 300 pupils became eligible, as we have seen, in November 1989. This gives a total of over 25,000 schools, with 7 million pupils. By 1 April 1991 a total of 194 parental ballots had been held, nineteen in primary schools. Of these the majority – 148 – voted to opt out, 46 against. Of those voting to opt out, about half were facing the threat of closure or reorganisation.

On 1 April 1991 a total of 62 GMSs were operating. By mid-July the total reached 100 in England and Wales. As LSI point out, this means that 0.4 per cent of all eligible schools had gained GMS status by that date. LSI goes on to state, however, that the Secretary of State has announced that if the Conservatives win the general election he expects GMS status to become the norm. 'This would completely change the present education system established by the 1944 Act.'[30]

LSI has also calculated the cost to the Exchequer of mass opting out – on the new funding levels. This amounts to £4.2 billion. This figure dramatically reveals the extent of the financial incentive this government is prepared to offer to achieve their purposes: though whether it would be maintained is another (political) question.

Later developments, in the early summer of 1991, may be briefly summarised. The *Times Educational Supplement* reported in May that very few primary schools had been tempted to opt out – a total of nine schools had actually applied for GMS status while a further ten had voted to do so, but still had to submit applications. Ballots were pending in 25 more primary schools, but LSI reported few enquiries. This is in spite of the fact that small primaries would gain over £20,000 plus £30 per pupil as 'transitional grant', as well as a capital allocation of £19,000 plus £9 per pupil (more for larger schools). The conclusion was that primary schools didn't appear to want this money.[31] In the meantime increasingly confident, or aggressive, statements by Kenneth Clarke, which will be referred to shortly, sparked an alarmed response from the Churches and local authorities in London. A joint statement from the Anglican diocese in London and the Anglican and Roman Catholic dioceses of Southwark, with the Association of Metropolitan Authorities (AMA) pointed out that the government had not even consulted the Churches over the changes planned in the Local Government Review. The director of education in the Archdiocese of Southwark told the managers of Catholic schools that to opt out from local control would be politically inopportune and morally questionable.[32] Early in April the education chairman of a 'staunchly Conservative borough' (Bromley) resigned in protest at the government's opting out policy, holding that it would leave Bromley pupils without secondary places and would lower standards. The idea, he held, 'has not been properly thought out'.[33]

In the meantime the chief government spokesman, Kenneth Clarke, escalated his public statements on this issue. Speaking to the Secondary Heads Association at the end of March he said that GMS status was a natural extension of LMS. Shortly after announcing the 'relaxation' of the five-year rule preventing grant maintained schools

from changing their status (which negated a guarantee consistently and strongly pressed by Kenneth
Baker), he added, 'What I am utterly convinced of is
that grant maintained status will become the norm.
Numbers have doubled in a year.'[34] He also now
announced his support for greater rewards for 'super
teachers' in grant maintained schools – yet another
differentiating factor.

At about this time, the new requirement that local
authorities should stump up a total of 16 per cent
extra funding for grant maintained schools (seen as
their proportion of local authority services and
administrative expenses) was leading to financial
crises in some areas. Late in June (1991) it was
reported that the London borough of Hillingdon,
where half the secondary schools were planning to
opt out, had been forced to 'restructure' their
administrative and back-up system to make the
money (£700,000) available to the schools.[35] Shortly
after, Labour councillors at Ealing appealed to the
government to reject plans from eight schools to opt
out. This would have serious financial consequences
for the 94 schools of the borough since the authority
would lose about £2 million from its education
budget.[36] Statistics produced at this time showed
that opting out was proving disproportionately
popular in *Conservative* areas; one interpretation of
this was that opting out 'is a vote of no confidence in
the underfunding of education in those areas'.[37]
Martin Rogers, of LSI, when asked what parents
voting for GMS status were actually voting *for*,
replied:

> Money, mainly, but they haven't the faintest idea what
> the future holds for them outside the LEA system.
> Nobody has. Very few of them actually believe the

education system will be better in five years time than it is today.[38]

Much the same point was made by the general secretary of the Society of Education Officers. The opting out figures, he said, bore out the warnings that they have been trying to communicate to ministers.

> It underlines the fact the parents are voting for money and responding to the carrots which the government has been offering – in many cases with very little regard for long-term improvements for the education system. The additional funds now being made available to encourage opting out make a nonsense of the principle of fairness of funding and reduce the ability of LEAs to provide a full range of support services to the other schools.[39]

To the amazement of the educational world, early in August 1991 the Prime Minister, in a letter to the secretary of the NUT, suddenly announced that (in spite of reiterated and consistent denials by ministers and officials),

> We have made no secret of the fact that grant maintained schools get preferential treatment in allocating grants to capital expenditure. We look favourably at grant maintained schools to encourage the growth of the sector, and I am delighted to see numbers are continuing to grow rapidly.[40]

By this means, one must suppose, the charge of bribery is to be dispelled. But what other word is appropriate?

There can be no question whatever that the opting

out legislation of the 1988 Act represents the greatest and most immediate threat to the existing education system as we know it. This is because, if opting out becomes universal, education authorities will be left with no serious role whatever. The schools, in this dispensation, will be controlled from the centre, by the DES, whatever intermediate agency the government sets up to carry out their behests. On this specific issue there is a very clear difference between the policy of the Labour Party on the one hand (and the Liberal Democrats) and of the Tories on the other. It is now abundantly clear that the latter want *all* schools to opt out. The Labour Party's policy, agreed at the 1990 conference, is to allow no more opting out and to return existing grant maintained schools to the local authority system as a matter of urgency. Labour's Secretary of State, it has been announced, would personally assume immediate control of the grants to grant maintained schools.[41]

City Technology Colleges

The city technology college programme, as indicated earlier (pp. 59-64) appears, on the other hand, to have run into the sand. Government representatives, however, continue to go through the motions of hyping this initiative as opportunity offers. So, in May 1991, announcing plans for two more CTCs, at Kingswood (Bristol) and in Derby, Kenneth Clarke claimed that these would be, 'like those already open, a resounding success as centres for excellence and demonstrating new methods of delivering high standards of education'.[42] For the Kingswood CTC the DES is providing £8 million (of taxpayers' money). This news, as in all such cases, met an unfavourable response from those responsible for local schools. This is 'bad news for Kingswood schools', said Edward Watson, Avon's deputy director. 'With the money spent on the CTC every secondary school in the area could be repaired and given a new science lab. In addition, every primary school could have an additional nursery class.'[43] The same point was made by the head of Haberdasher's Aske's Hatcham girls' school a month earlier. A parliamentary answer had revealed that a total of £5 million of taxpayers' money had been allotted to the proposed Haberdasher's CTC. In the same LEA (Lewisham) discussions were taking place on the effects of the cuts in education which would need to be implemented if the authority was to avoid rate-capping. These amounted to £5 million. 'What further proof', the head asked, 'is necessary to display the unfairness of the CTC programme?'[44]

Macabre developments continued to be reported in this field. Late in May 1991 the *Guardian* claimed that the government stood to lose 'at least £300,000' in a land sale after plans to set up a CTC in Brighton collapsed; apparently the sponsors, having bought the site for £2.3 million, succeeded in selling it to the government for £2.5 million. The lost £200,000, it is reported, was recovered, but that there would be a considerable net loss to the government on the whole unfortunate transaction seems clear.[45] At roughly this point the financial columns of the quality press were full of the doings of Michael Ashcroft, chairman of ADT, described in the *Independent* as the City's *enfant terrible* – or, in the *Observer*, as 'the man the City loves to hate'.[46] According to the latter report, Kenneth Baker 'persuaded Ashcroft to stump up most of the £1.7 million needed to fund a city technology college in

Wandsworth' (see pp. 61-4). Ashcroft's affairs, closely linked to the Conservative Party, are too complex to enter into here but, as a result of a series of financial crises, 'he seemingly decided to take himself out of Britain, whether for tax or other purposes'. His yacht was moved offshore to the Guernsey register, and 'even last December's statutory meeting of the Wandsworth CTC board was held somewhere in Europe'.

Although what might be called the 'classic' CTC project (twenty colleges) is clearly not to be extended (and probably not reached), pressure from the Tory right seems to have been effective in reviving Cyril Taylor's voluntary-aided alternative, already discussed earlier (pp. 63-4). Rumours suddenly abounded about this as premature pre-election fever mounted early in June 1991. The *Times Educational Supplement* in fact announced at the end of June that this plan had been 'abandoned', quoting Kenneth Clark as telling industrialists that legislation required to legitimise this initiative was *not* going ahead – Wandsworth had been forced to abandon plans for a voluntary-aided CTC as a result of these difficulties, while a DES letter to a trust concerned with such a school at Lincoln informed them that the legal (and financial) problems posed rendered the plan 'insuperable at this point in time'.[47] A fortnight later, however, the same journal reported the government's firm intention 'to breathe new life into the CTC programme' by allowing local authority, grant-maintained *and* voluntary aided schools to become 'technical colleges'.[48] In a major speech on education – hosted, significantly, by the Centre for Policy Studies (a right-wing grouping) – the Prime Minister in fact promised to legislate 'to remove the technical and legal obstacles that stand in the way of those voluntary-aided schools that wish to become city technology colleges'. And here yet another top-down initiative was suddenly launched on the educational world. 'We will go one step further creating another new type of school,' said John Major.

> We will enable existing schools to transform themselves into grant-maintained technology colleges, incorporating the key characteristics of the CTCs – focus on technical education, support from private sector sponsors.[49]

Amplifying this announcement, Kenneth Clark said that the proposed legislation would overcome the legal obstacles preventing local authority involvement (its high degree of financial involvement under the law at present). The proposed legislation would enable local authorities to set up and maintain these colleges alongside private industry.

Sir Cyril Taylor of the CTC trust was (unsurprisingly) reported as looking forward 'enthusiastically to setting up a dozen voluntary-aided CTCs' in the wake of the promised legislation. Baroness Cox was also delighted, as also Donald Naismith, Wandsworth's CEO (and apparently an adviser to John Major). All this, commented *Education*, indicates 'the degree to which the right wing of the Conservative Party believes they have won the battle for Mr Major's ear on education policy'.[50] This speech of the Prime Minister's will be referred to again later.

So ... the future is unclear. New initiatives abound and their, often quite casual, announcement all add to the current uncertainty. In the meantime public concern is being widely expressed on moral and financial issues relating to the existing CTCs. In July 1991 the Prime Minister visited the Harris CTC at Norwood, South London. The new school, the *Guardian* claimed, was being funded exceptionally generously – at the level of £2.67 million per annum (covering recurrent expenditure). With 757 pupils, that level of funding is £1 million per annum *more* than a normal school would get (according to the *Guardian*). In addition this school was due to receive further substantial tranches of public money for specific purposes. Derek Fatchett, Labour's education representative, objected to the 'double standards' operated by the government: 'This is public money and Ministers cannot treat CTCs like a private fiefdom.' The NUT also objected to the unwillingness of the government to reveal 'the true level of spending' (the government had refused to reveal the extent of funding for the Norwood school). According to the *Guardian* all government offices, including the DES which 'would not even confirm' the Harris figures, clammed up on this issue.[51] A fortnight later this paper returned again to this question, heading their report 'City Technology Colleges Funding Belies Equality Claim'. Pupils at city technology colleges 'will attract up to £185 a head more in public funds than those at neighbouring local authority schools', the *Guardian* argued, based on government figures just released. This conflicts with assurances previously given that, once established, 'CTC running costs a pupil paid by the government will be similar to those in council maintained schools in similar catchment areas.' Ministers are reported as saying that the extra money being paid to the colleges (now apparently admitted) covers 'diseconomies of scale' during each college's start-up period, but local authorities dispute 'that such sums are also available to new schools under their control'.[52]

Whatever the truth of all this, the scenario relating to both these institutions, GMSs and CTCs, and especially what Derek Fatchett has called the 'substantial sweeteners' provided,[53] appears to reflect something of the government's desperation to get these initiatives off the ground almost at whatever cost. That cost is, of course, provided at the expense of the public system which, under a different dispensation, could have benefitted. Further, the first serious research study of a CTC, by Geoffrey Walford and Henry Miller, on the Kingshurst School at Solihull – while sympathetic to the work of the school in many respects, concludes negatively.[54] The CTCs, the authors argue, 'cannot engage in any meaningful way with most of the real and perceived problems and tasks that have been set for them'. They do not begin to tackle inner-city problems (for which they were established, according to Baker's rhetoric), 'nor can they do very much to improve technical and vocational education'. Indeed,

> It is only in privatisation, selection and differentiation of provision according to the existing social order, that the CTCs actually begin to engage with the issues, and they have done so in a socially regressive way.

The whole initiative was misconceived. The authors conclude that

> What is important is that the expensive facilities and good practice that are evident in some of the CTCs are not lost, and that the distracting, disrupting and counter-productive effects arising from the ideological manner in which they were established is overcome.

This is best done 'by bringing the CTCs within the LEA framework such that *all* children in the area can benefit'.

Curriculum and Assessment

In the last chapter I argued that the various measures embodied in the Education Act must be understood in their inter-relations, and that the whole comprises an ingenious package directed to shifting the whole direction of public education, subjecting its operation to market forces while at the same time reinforcing direct control at all key points (the Act gave some 300 new powers to the Secretary of State). On this interpretation, the curriculum and assessment measures now brought in are central to the operation of the Act as a whole. It is from this angle that the analysis will be pursued in this essay, the argument elaborated and its implications considered.

The Baker-Thatcher rhetoric, 'power to the parents', by which the government sought popular support for this measure, was not intended (originally, at least) to apply to what the parents' offspring actually did at school. On the contrary, all were to study the same set of subjects from the age of five to sixteen for some 85 per cent of the time (as originally proposed); further, not only were these subjects to be studied, all pupils in all maintained schools were to be subjected to assessment (including 'nationally prescribed tests') at the ages of seven, eleven, fourteen and sixteen.

Such precise determination of children's activity over eleven years is certainly unique in Britain. However that may be, and for whatever reasons so draconian a system was thought necessary, it had one implication which tied it in closely to the structural features of the Act: as argued in Chapter 6, it was *the* condition making possible the wholesale devolution of financial responsibility for individual schools on to the newly constituted governing bodies now dominated by parents (in place of local authority representatives). The schools could now be seen as autonomous institutions, 'liberated' from direct local authority control. But every school had a legal obligation to toe the curriculum line laid down centrally, and indeed, in the last resort, in the control of the Secretary of State. This means that no single school could step out of line and pursue quite other directions; that clear conditions for the maintenance of control over the school's functioning had been achieved. This was the condition for LMS. It was, therefore, also the essential condition without which the objective of creating market conditions in education could not have been achieved.

It is not, of course, being suggested that this was the sole reason for the introduction of the national curriculum – only that the gradual move in this direction made it possible to fit it neatly into the package that was ERA. Government representatives, especially Baker, stressed the contribution it would make in raising standards generally, focusing also on the need for breadth and on the need to ensure the achievement of minimum levels of attainment. Further, a standard curriculum of this kind, together with pupil assessment, would provide parents with data helpful to facilitating parental choice, would minimise disruption caused by changing schools (mobility), while 'formative assessment' would be supportive of individual pupils' progress. There were some, as we have seen, who, basing themselves on the long-term teacher pressure for a common curriculum within the comprehensive school, saw the national curriculum as essentially defining an entitlement for all.

Assessment is defined as an essential aspect of the National Curriculum in the Education Act itself – and perhaps rightly so, in that the form and actuality of assessment will drive, or underlie, the teaching. As stressed elsewhere in this volume, the major, long-term social significance of the form assessment is to take in England and Wales rests in the fact that the entire child population, as it emerges from the schools at the age of sixteen, will be categorised in terms of the ten levels originally proposed in the TGAT (Task Group for Assessment and Testing) report (and accepted by the government). As suggested earlier (in Chapter 4), the distribution of pupils among these levels is likely to assume the form of the normal or Gauss curve, with the bulk grouped around the mean; level 10 at sixteen is apparently to be equated only with the top half of those gaining Grade A in GCSE, level 7 being equivalent to the present grade C while level 4 reflects a minimum GCE pass. The implications of this categorisation of the entire youthful population will be a matter for the Brave New World of the twenty-first century.

It is clear enough that the National Curriculum, and assessment, are here to stay – though not necessarily in their present form, indeed recent developments, referred to later, suggest otherwise. Neither the Labour Party nor the Liberal Democrats, however, are at present proposing any radical changes, and both accept the need for such measures. One of the features of the present situation is the speed with which the whole transformation is taking place. One informed comment points out that this transformation, whereby 'apart from matters of relatively small detail and individual teaching style, everything is to be prescribed from the centre', could hardly be directly imposed from the centre.[55] Eschewing pure imposition, the government and the DES opted to go through the normal full consultation process 'at both macro and micro levels'. Indeed all this was included in the Education Act. 'But uniquely', Cashden and Wilson go on, 'they also decided to do this at a lightning speed. So the total time-scale for a complete change over of the school system, virtually from initial conception to final and complete implementation, is under ten years.' The result has been that real consultation periods (for instance, over the curriculum Working Party reports) 'have often been in weeks, rather than months, never in years'. Class teachers have consequently been over-burdened 'simply keeping up to date with requirements' – in English alone, 'teachers at primary level are recommended to read ten reports, most of them quite hefty'.

Another result has been a series of retreats by the government from the full original concept of the National Curriculum. In February 1991 Kenneth Clarke announced that new regulations being considered would allow subjects other than English, maths and science to be dropped, or rendered optional, at fourteen. New short-term vocational courses were to be introduced; all this in spite of the fact that the National Curriculum Council was about to come up with a viable plan covering these years.[56] At this period also several decisions by the Secretary of State were characterised as politically motivated, or, in the case of the science decisions, as 'a cynical political exercise'.[57] More recently the edict has gone forth that 'history' stops at 1960, though Welsh history stops earlier (in 1900), so effectively excluding study by Welsh pupils of the turbulent history of industrial confrontations which marked South Wales throughout the twentieth century. The problems with assessment at Key Stage 1 (seven-year-olds) made the national press for six months or more, while in Scotland the mass refusal of parents to allow their children to be examined has totally disrupted the programme.[58] As a result Key Stage 1 assessment virtually collapsed – there is now to be no formal assessment at all in the foundation subjects other than those in the 'core' (maths, science, English). It is now likely that similar decisions will be taken as regards Key Stage 2 (eleven-year-olds), though the teachers will still have to make and record their own assessments in the other foundation subjects. As I write, the Key Stage 3 assessment procedures are in a state of more or less total confusion, with the Secretary of State publicly (and characteristically) condemning the proposed pilot tests in science and mathematics as 'elaborate nonsense', leading to widespread speculation that Kenneth Clarke was 'planning to dismiss both his curriculum and examination advisers' and substitute a new single body.[59] In May 1991 Clarke announced that the maths and science tests for fourteen-year-olds are to be delayed a year (until 1993), following the government's decision to simplify syllabuses.[60]

Not only is the National Curriculum itself in the years fourteen to sixteen to be severely modified, or weakened (in terms of unity and breadth), but controversy over teacher supply, especially in the field of science, remains sharp and bitter. For instance, three prestigious bodies, headed by the Royal Society, on reporting that the dearth of science teachers promises to persist, and that nearly one in four teaching the subject admits to insufficient knowledge and experience to do so, found the Secretary of State airily dismissing their findings as 'self-interested moaning'. 'I query the scientific accuracy of this particular scientific criticism,' he said on the radio, earning a severe rebuke from the main leader in the *Times Educational Supplement* – those assisting ministers to meet their objectives 'are entitled to expect courtesy and consideration for their efforts rather than arrogant bluster'.[61] With these attitudes, the outlook for delivery of an effective entitlement curriculum to all seems increasingly remote.

The July Events

In fact, over the rest of the summer of 1991 (and in July in particular) the pace of change suddenly hotted up. Now John Major, as Prime Minister, began to play a leading role while hostile confrontation between education ministers and representatives of local government escalated to an unprecedented degree. At the same time important changes in personnel once again swung the balance towards the Tories' radical right. Just before the summer recess these and like developments once again left the educational world in a condition of stunned bewilderment. One thing became very clear – the goal posts were again to be moved.

What sparked this new activity must be a matter for future historians to unravel. One interpretation, which seems likely to be near the truth, links these developments to the premature pre-election fever which dominated the media in July. Faced with the possibility of a quick election, the Conservative Party was now determined to articulate 'a set of easy-to-digest educational policies' which might be propagated through the proposed Citizen's Charter, and later elaborated in a Parents' Charter.[62] References were made in the press at this time to John Major's desire 'to seize the initiative in education', involving substantial modification, or total jettisoning, of the TGAT assessment scheme, as well as other matters. There was to be a firm hand at the helm, the Prime Minister's; his involvement was intended, presumably, to symbolise the government's commitment to a populist revision of educational change.

That there were grounds for the government's concern is clear. Already early in June it was reported that the Prime Minister was disturbed at the evidence from opinion polls showing 'cynicism over the effect of recent reforms' in the public services; he was, therefore, anxious to recover the initiative as an innovator in these fields'.[63] Striking confirmation of declining public support was provided by a Gallup poll early in July. This showed that, by a majority of two to one, people disapproved of government changes and thought they would make education worse. Tory support as the best party to handle education, reported Demitri Coryton, 'has fallen back to the 25 per cent level that it was at for most of last year'. In contrast to the Tories' figure, Labour gained a 49 per cent response as the 'best party', and the Liberal Democrats scored 11 per cent. To the question 'Do you broadly approve or broadly disapprove of the changes currently taking place in the way the education system is run?', responses showed that 22 per cent approved,

53 per cent disapproved, while 25 per cent 'didn't know'. The author's conclusion was that Labour enjoys 'a substantial lead on education'. Further, the poll revealed that the number of people who think education rated as 'a major problem' had substantially risen during the year. These figures

> suggest that Kenneth Clarke has failed to get his message across. Or, if he has succeeded, the public do not like the message. On these figures there is little public support for what he is trying to do.[64]

The first act in these new initiatives took place early in June – when a group of 'experts' were summoned at short notice to John Major's 'citizen's summit' at Chequers, 'to thrash out "eye-catching ideas" for improvement of the public services'. Education, it was reported, was to be 'a centre-piece of the charter now being prepared', and this would lead to 'further legislation' if the Conservatives win the next general election, and be embodied in their manifesto. The 'main talking point' was 'standards', the contributors being Mrs Pauline Perry (later ennobled), Donald Naismith (CEO for Wandsworth) and Howard Davies (Controller of the Audit Commission). At this meeting the Prime Minister is reported as saying that there should be 'much greater emphasis on efficiency and consumer satisfaction'; that more needed to be done to 'demystify' standards. The Citizen's Charter was likely to emphasise 'simpler and better communication to the public of national assessment results based on standardised tests rather than the current Standard Assessment Tasks' (SATs) which were radically criticised by the 'experts'. This, the report runs, 'could mean the virtual scrapping of the Black

Report on testing and assessment [the TGAT report, B.S.] on which the current National Curriculum is based'. Background papers at this conference also suggested the actual *abolition* of local authority inspectorates as being too 'producer-dominated'. Participants left Chequers apparently in no doubt 'that the Prime Minister wishes to set his own policy direction in the public services'.[65]

The next (logical) step was the delivery of the Prime Minister's first important speech on education already referred to. It surely has significance that the platform deliberately chosen was a conference organised by the Centre for Policy Studies, well known as a leading think-tank of the radical right within the Conservative Party. In many ways, this was a sharply aggressive, politically partisan speech, announcing several new policy initiatives. Here Major promised to repay parents the cost of campaign expenses in promoting opting out, and to curb the amount that LEAs could spend 'in trying to prevent it'. He announced his anxiety to increase the number of grant maintained schools in inner city areas, and the new type of grant-maintained CTCs mentioned earlier (p. 170). 'We need new institutions to break the mould of political extremism and bureaucratic inefficiency which too often characterises the inner city areas,' he intoned (without citing the culprits). 'I'm sure the grant-maintained concept will win hearts and minds in every community.'[66]

On examinations and assessment, Major repeated his firm commitment to retaining existing GCE A levels in their present form, saying that GCSE exams must be modified to fit (or lead on to) these, rather than vice versa. There was, he proclaimed, 'far too much coursework' in GCSE, which must be revised to become once more an externally-assessed, 'predominantly written' exam. Course work must be limited to a maximum of 20 per cent.[67] Tests, at seven, eleven, fourteen and sixteen, he added, are here to stay. 'We must be able to measure children's progress in an objective and regular manner.' We need, however, 'to shift the emphasis towards shorter, standardised tests, which the whole class can take at one time'. Major also outlined some of the propositions for the Citizen's Charter, to be published later in July, including 'better and more complete information to parents about schools and more rigorous inspections and comprehensive reports to parents'. He concluded with a sharp attack on 'the left' and, as has been obligatory for some time with Conservative politicians, on the 1960s generally (the two are equated). The left was contaminated by 'its mania for equality' – a mania 'that undermined common sense values in schools, rejected proven teaching methods – or disposed of them altogether'. This was 'a canker in our education system which spread from the 1960s on, and deprived great cohorts of our children of the opportunities they deserved'.[68]

There were a number of responses from the educational world to the Prime Minister's speech. Stuart Maclure (ex-editor of the *Times Educational Supplement*) was particularly shocked at the cavalier treatment accorded to A levels and GCSE. All are now agreed, he claimed, 'that A levels must be overhauled to provide a broader basis for higher education'. But not, apparently, John Major.

It really is deplorable that the Prime Minister of this country on a rare excursion into educational policy, should reduce a critically important discussion to a few tendentious slogans.

He should 'consult beyond the coteries of the radical Right'.[69] A week later, in a forthright open letter, Fred Jarvis, until recently Secretary of the National Union of Teachers, published a clear challenge on many of the issues raised by the Prime Minister. He concluded by asking whether the Prime Minister had any conception

> of the effect on the teachers' morale of all the upheavals, additional burdens and changes of course which the government has imposed; the denigration to which the profession and the LEAs have been subjected, and the lack of consultation and contempt for partnership which have characterised the government's approach to educational change.[70]

Tempers were rising.

But clearly the change in direction now determined on at the Chequers meetings, reinforced by Major's speech, would lead to new confrontations – and now centrally with the two bodies specifically brought into being by the 1988 Education Act to oversee, and 'advise' on, the National Curriculum and its attendant examinations and assessment procedures – the National Curriculum Council (NCC) and the Schools Examinations and Assessment Council (SEAC). All members of both these bodies had been directly appointed by the Secretary of State, both chairmen, Duncan Graham and Philip Halsey, being personally chosen by Kenneth Baker and approved by 10 Downing Street (Thatcher). Both chairs of these bodies also acted as chief executives, and both, from all accounts, dominated their respective committees, if in different ways. Both, of course, had built their procedures on the original TGAT report, which outlined a model of the curriculum, attainment targets and accompanying

SATs – indeed it was the sheer reasonableness of this report which ensured, at a crucial moment, that the Education 'Reform' Bill was made acceptable (in these respects) to the teaching profession generally. But, as we have seen, as the government (and/or ministers) began to move in directions opposite to that report's recommendations, particularly as concerns testing, increasingly sharp differences between these bodies (and so, their chairs) and ministers became not only observable but common knowledge.[71] Now that the Prime Minister had entered the fray, supporting radically rightist views on all these issues, the stage was set for confrontation. A bid was now to be made to assert direct (political) control over both these agencies which the government clearly wished to bring into line in support of the now transformed policies.

So, in mid-July, we had the sudden 'retirement' of the chairs (and chief executives) of *both* these organisations – first, that of Duncan Graham of the NCC, and, a week later, that of Philip Halsey of SEAC. Both could be said to be 'educationalists' – the former an ex-CEO, the latter a civil servant from the DES. Both were replaced, in their chairing roles, by party political nominees – Graham (NCC) by David Pascall, a former member of Thatcher's policy unit at Downing Street (and an industrialist); Halsey (SEAC) by Lord Griffiths, described as 'the right-wing economist who headed Margaret Thatcher's policy unit at No. 10 until her resignation', and appointed chairman of the right-wing Centre for Policy Studies in February 1991.[72] It is interesting (ominous?) to note that, according to the *Times Educational Supplement*, the order to remove Halsey came from 'political advisers to John Major, and not from Education Ministers'.[73]

Graham's resignation from the NCC, according to the *Times Educational Supplement*, followed disagreements between that body and Kenneth Clarke over the shape of the national curriculum.[74] Earlier in the year, as we have seen, Clarke ignored the NCC's advice on the crucial Key Stage 4 (fourteen to sixteen) while, the journal reported, Graham 'has [since] made no secret of resenting the heavy hand of ministers who had increasingly sidelined the NCC and SEAC ignoring recommendations and overturning decisions'.[75] The announcement of Graham's resignation, following Major's speech the previous week, came at a time when the National Curriculum and testing 'appear to be undergoing radical revision'. Commenting a week later on Halsey's resignation, two years early, the *Independent* asserted that he opposed 'simple tests at seven', and that he was also unhappy about the Prime Minister's proposal to reduce coursework in GCSE. Now the heads of the two school bodies have gone, continued the report, 'the government will find it easier to merge the two councils and make them more responsive to ministers' demands'.[76]

Griffiths' first task, commented the *Guardian*, 'is to respond to John Major's demand for pencil and paper testing that can be done by a class all at one time'.[77] He would also re-write the rules for testing at fourteen and preserve the 'integrity' of A levels. As chair of the Centre for Policy Studies, Griffiths 'strongly supported' Major's speech on testing, and was generally a severe critic of 'egalitarian' approaches. When at 10 Downing Street Griffiths is said to have gathered 'a coterie of advisers' which included the ubiquitous Donald Naismith, Clare Burstall (director, NFER), Stuart Sexton, Peter Dawson (PAT) and others. His views on education, according to Nick Tester (deputy editor of *Education*), 'are simplistic and on exams Neanderthal. He comes to the job with only a briefcase full of prejudices to draw on.'[78]

Once Major had taken the decision, reported the *Times Educational Supplement* at the end of this torrid month, Kenneth Clarke was in a position to appoint new heads – for SEAC, NCC *and* HMI (where the Chief Inspector, George Bolton, had recently resigned).[79] These are 'the three key educational agencies influencing schools'. No official explanation was given for Halsey's resignation (SEAC); he had done a good job and was supported by his staff. Duncan Graham, however, had operated in a more dictatorial way. His successor as chair, Pascall, 'had been one of the main critics' of his style of leadership, and had even led a delegation of ministers to protest at this. George Low, editor of *Education*, reported that the group of new right-wing members of the NCC, appointed (with Pascall) a year earlier, 'ganged up on Duncan'. If so, they gained their reward ('he was brutal but effective').[80]

These changes of key personnel, and especially the sudden disappearance of leading figures, were received with consternation. On Griffiths' appointment in place of Halsey, Jack Straw commented that this was 'a vulgar and partisan abuse of power by Mr Clarke'. The effect, he added, 'is almost certainly to undermine confidence in the national curriculum'.[81] The strongest expression of distaste, however, came from a neutral source, a main leader in the *Times Educational Supplement*. Entitled 'Time to Stop the Rubbishing', this asserted that we had now entered 'a period of pre-election high fever, with education cast as prime target for the Prime Minister's nostrums'. It was now clear that education was considered too important to be left to the Education Secretary, so John Major had stepped in. There was a need to promise instant change before a possible November election 'has become the overriding imperative'.

> It is an unbelievable way to run an education service ... quite apart from the confusion caused to schools, teachers and parents by the current spate of edicts, sound-bites, and hirings and firings, to treat so shabbily people who have contributed so much will not encourage talented people to devote their lives to this branch of public service.

The government, the *Times Education Supplement* concluded, 'has certainly lost patience or confidence in its own reforms'.[82]

Early in August Paul Black, architect of TGAT, was removed from his membership, and as deputy chair, of the NCC.[83] The clear-out was complete. Outcomes (of all these changes of personnel) would no doubt become apparent from the autumn of 1991.

But, in the meantime, the government's (or rather the Conservative Party's) machine ground on. Already at the end of July the Citizen's Charter – hurriedly concocted as we have seen – was published; the subsequent Parent's Charter, which would set out parents' rights, was now promised for September. The Citizen's Charter had a mixed reception – as far as schools were concerned it contained little that was in fact new. The Audit Commission was to publish comparative tables on local authority efficiency; from 1991-92 all schools, further education colleges and sixth form colleges would be required to publish annual examination results; schools must also publish truancy levels and other items (to be defined later); comparative information on all schools must be collected and published locally; all pupils would receive a school report annually including test results; local authorities must publish 'summary comparative results from local schools in local newspapers'. Most of these measures were prefigured in the original ERA consultation papers (see pp. 135-6). There was, however, one new and important policy announcement. This concerned the regular inspection of schools, which is to be a statutory requirement (involving legislation). It presages the actual abolition of the existing local authority inspectorate (or advisory staff), although it does not actually say so. This item also has links with the poll tax imbroglio since it involves expenditure by central government instead of by local authorities. The Charter announced that 'A specific grant will be paid directly to schools to enable them to buy inspections with a corresponding reduction in revenue support grants to LEAs.' The choice of 'inspectors' is to be left with governing bodies.[84]

The bulk of the proposals concerned the publication of league tables. The Prime Minister, commented *Education*, is seeking more value for money, without significant extra public expenditure. Many of the educational recommendations are 'old hat'.[85] The National Council of Parent Teacher Associations (NCPTA), pointing out that it had not been consulted, regarded many of the measures embodied in the Charter as 'misguided'. The NCPTA's recent national conference had rejected the whole concept of the publication of league tables as now proposed in the Charter.[86] Apparently impervious to the mounting criticism from various quarters, Kenneth Clarke now informed teachers in Liverpool that he believed the education service had turned a corner and that 'The education revolution had bedded down.' 'It has been a hard slog,' he added, 'and there have been times when people must have thought that the whole edifice would come crashing down.'[87] But by this time this was clearly what most people were thinking.

In the meantime those concerned with the actual 'delivery' of the education service – local authorities and their chief officials – now at last were becoming increasingly alarmed about Tory policies in education and their effect. At their annual conference held at Belfast at the end of June, Chief Education Officers and other officials expressed concern at the 'piecemeal dismantling of the service'; government policies would lead to 'a disintegration' of education and to 'greater inequality between schools'. The CEOs, it was reported, were now to abandon their traditional non-political stance and publicly campaign against the policies of the government. A statement now drafted for publication presented the views of the membership.

> The government's attachment to market forces as a way of determining the quality of schools and colleges would mean better provision for the few at the cost of equality of access for all pupils.

Education, it was held, had become over-politicised. A representative from Hillingdon, a Tory authority, warned that the problems created by opting out could lead to the end of the local education service.[88]

Another report stressed that the Society of Education Officers (SEO) now committed itself to resisting what it saw as 'the steady erosion in the vision of an entitlement to good quality education for the whole community'. In the SEO's view,

Recent reforms aimed at unleashing market forces on the educational system threatened not only the future of public education but also the economy and civilisation of the country.

There was evidence from Kent and elsewhere that support services for schools were beginning to disintegrate, while the proposed removal of Further Education from LEA control induced a sense of despair. Delegates, ran the report, gave expression to 'their pent-up exasperation with government policy and how it promises to destroy local authorities as we know them'. This conference concluded by demanding from their officers 'strong and instant statements to counter the rubbishing of education that keeps happening at the hands of politicians'.[89]

But by now other organisations representing local authorities, including those under Conservative control, were up in arms. Early in July the Tory-controlled Association of County Councils 'bitterly attacked' government plans for the control of Further Education to pass from local authorities to what they called 'undemocratic quangos'. These will create 'a centralised bureaucracy with no local government element' and were, therefore, thoroughly to be deplored.[90] 'Tory shires of south England are girding themselves for battle,' thundered the *Daily Telegraph* at the end of the month. The general election was looming and the stakes had never been higher. 'It is not fear that the government will be thrown out that haunts them, but the prospect that it will be returned.'[91] The chairs of nine shire counties were planning a joint appeal to Downing Street.

The confrontation between central and local

government reached a high point at the Conference of Local Education Authorities (CLEA) in mid-July, deliberately fuelled by sharply aggressive speeches by a junior minister, Tim Eggar. Apparently Eggar felt that the best policy now was to turn on the heat, which he did in no uncertain manner, provoking oppositional jeers of disgust. Local authorities, he said, 'are bringing themselves into disrepute by an obstructive attitude towards schools opting out of their control', they are (he added), 'on probation for the future running of schools'. Many local authorities still regard grant maintained schools and city technology colleges 'with hostility or suspicion' and engage in 'petty obstruction'. 'Such doctrinaire attitudes are an anachronism.'[92]

But at a private meeting at the CLEA conference with representatives of Tory authorities, the second junior minister, Michael Fallon, is reported to have suffered an hour-and-a-half's unremitting hostility 'from his own people'. Those working in local government are, it was reported, 'at best disoriented and at worst demoralised'. Phillip Merridale, until recently chairman of the Hampshire Education Committee, said his party's structural reforms of late 'were haphazard and lacking vision'. Labour representatives were outraged. Nicky Harrison, a respected and long-serving education committee chair, complained that current education ministers were 'arrogant and rude'. All present, it was reported – Labour, Conservative, Liberal Democrat or 'hung' (councils) recognised 'they all had a common enemy' – the government and in particular Kenneth Clarke. 'He is the most ill-regarded Secretary of State for education in living memory by those who actually run the system, the LEAs.'[93]

Tim Eggar took the opportunity to spell out the

implications of the Citizen's Charter at the CLEA conference. This implied more delegation, more opting out, more contracting out. More importantly, he now drove home to local authorities that their responsibility for quality assurance was to be removed. The money for inspection was to go direct to the schools. Other functions were also to go:

> Local government does not have a natural monopoly of responsibility for planning the future pattern of schools and colleges; nor does it have a natural monopoly in arrangements for inspection and quality assurance ... that philosophy belongs to a different era, it should be put aside. It places too much emphasis on the system and not enough on individual schools.[94]

Nor was this all; yet a further blow awaited the CLEA delegates. Howard Davies, Controller of the Audit Commission and an adviser to the Prime Minister on the Citizen's Charter, now warned the conference 'that the full fall-out of the poll tax had not yet been felt. Even more functions might be removed from local government to relieve the council tax-payer.'[95]

So the scene is set for further depredations.

There have been several assessments of the state of education in the late summer of 1991. These have come from various sources, but three in particular stand out – all from people who, one way or another, are relatively detached from current controversies.

Here is Lord Taylor's assessment, made in a journal for parents and school governors.[96] It was Lord Taylor who chaired the committee which first proposed revision of governing bodies and substantial representation for parents.[97] School governors, he claims, have been misled by the government into thinking they can raise standards. But central government spending cuts and the poll tax have squeezed schools, hitting provision of school meals, the national curriculum, special needs and teachers' jobs.

> Thus parents and governors have come bitterly to resent being given responsibility without the means to exercise it, and the blame for cuts which are the last they would willingly agree to. Governors find themselves with cruel choices which are far from the promised joys of a chance to make real contributions to better schools. The process which has made parents and governors the instruments of the government's parsimonious and divisive policies must be ended. I should be very sorry if my committee's hard work had merely dragged well meaning and caring people into the task of dismantling education as a sharing and caring service, meeting needs and providing new opportunities for *all* children, and turning it instead into a market place in which only the strong survive and that at the expense of their consciences.

In a sense, that says it all.

But here is Mary Warnock, chair of the committee which produced the report on children with special educational needs,[98] to which the 1981 Education Act was intended to give effect. The TES recently asked whether the Act was dead. ' "Stillborn", is the verdict of one of its progenitors, Mary Warnock, who had just written its valediction.' Its ideas were first savaged by cuts, then 'buried by the Thatcherite help-yourself values of the market-place'. Now the notion of pupils' needs has disappeared. For that would entail that in some cases more had to be spent on those whose needs were greatest; and this could never be cost-effective. The introduction of formula funding (LMS) has further disadvantaged the disadvantaged. The disabled and disadvantaged 'do not need "care": they need education on a basis of equal rights', Mary Warnock concludes. It is this which is at risk.[99]

And here is an 'end of term' report by Stephen Bates, the *Guardian*'s education editor:

> By any objective measure, the government's education policies have had a bad year. The national curriculum remains bogged down in bumf, the examinations system is producing 'elaborate nonsense', the city technology colleges plan has juddered to a halt, grant maintained schools are scarcely flooding in and the testing of seven-year-olds was a fiasco.[100]

In education, Bates continues, the government

> has politically resorted to the quick fix – bring in a bouncy new minister here, select more amenable advisers there, announce a few new initiatives with apparently large sums of money attached today, express outrage at falling standards tomorrow.

It is not surprising that ministers should have run out of ideas. 'What is surprising is that they seem to be going out of their way to alienate everyone remotely connected with the subject, including their own supporters.'

'By all accounts Mr Fallon's attempt to inspire the Tory troops from the shires at last week's local authority conference was a particularly ripe example, leaving them spitting blood.'

How, then, can we evaluate the overall situation as it appears in the early autumn of 1991? Is it the case, as predicted by Peter Wilby on election day in June 1987, that the return of a Tory government would lead to the break-up of the system which had existed since 1944? Or, as asked at the start of this chapter, are the measures now in place and being implemented 'on the way' to bringing about this break-up? Alternatively, has resistance over the last three years been successful in preserving (and building on) the main features of the earlier system?

There is no easy answer to these questions. It is clear, from the evidence cited in both this and the last chapter, that many in responsible positions fear that the crucial turning point has in fact already been reached. Those directly concerned with local government and its role are dismayed at what the Society of Education Officers see as 'the piecemeal dismantling of the service' and the steady and clearly deliberate erosion of local responsibilities. There appears to be a strong and almost desperate thrust from the centre to ensure direct control of all aspects of education and to cut erstwhile 'partners' – local authorities, teachers above all – down to size. This relates not only to the structure of the system as a whole but also to its content – in particular to the curriculum and to testing (and assessment). Here the really extraordinary coup d'etat of July relating to control of the NCC and SEAC appears symptomatic. These bodies also must be brought into line obediently to carry through ministerial behests, however controversial. Outcomes are already manifest in the recent decisions concerning pencil-and-paper testing for both seven- and eleven-year-olds. In these cases the sheer effrontery of the overt politicisation of control over key *educational* bodies is remarkable, and, incidentally, entirely without precedent in the world of educational politics.

Such measures are directed at strengthening the thrust of government policy. One aim of that policy, at least as originally defined by Margaret Thatcher, was to create new constituencies of support for the Conservative Party (as put earlier in this chapter, p. 144). But the evidence indicates very clearly that such constituencies have not only *not* been created, but that the educational policies of the government are exceptionally unpopular. This, it seems, lies behind some of the more desperate measures now being introduced – the hope that, somehow, public attitudes will 'flip' and the longed for public support actually materialise. But this is unlikely.

And there lies the hope for the future. A really decisive break with the past has not, in fact, been achieved. The full negative effect of LMS and Open Enrolment in introducing differentiation has yet to be felt. That engine can still be put in reverse. Opting out has not, as yet, disrupted the system, though it is on the way to doing so in some areas. This can also still be reversed. CTCs are generally an (expensive) irrelevance. The National Curriculum is still in place though severely modified – with positive policies it could still be transformed into 'good quality education for the whole community' (pp. 76-7). So, on all these dimensions, there is still hope.

A general election must (as I write) take place within the next eight or nine months. Whatever the outcome, the new government faces a situation characterised by confrontation, demoralisation, conflict on a level perhaps never experienced before by this country. Yet all agree that major advances in education right across the board are necessary both to enhance the quality of life in Britain and to restore the country's economic and industrial position generally. There will be much to be done, and to be undone. The aim must be to build on (and recognise) the positive work of the schools, the teachers, and the local authorities. To restore to teachers and others the initiatives that have been wrested from them, and to define a vision of the future which, through co-operative endeavour, may be achievable and achieved. In place of the doctrinaire reliance on market forces to shape the future, we must substitute joint, co-operative effort by all concerned to build an educational environment directed to realising the full potentialities of all our citizens, whatever their age, gender, race or social class. Such must be the objective.

Notes and References

1. *Independent*, 11 June 1987.
2. Brian Simon, *Bending the Rules*, London 1988, p. 19.
3. The Poll Tax, David Blunkett is reported as saying recently, 'is proving to be the most expensive and disastrous political experiment perpetrated on the British people in modern times', *Guardian*, 5 August 1991. He was commenting on revelations about the uncollectability of the tax.
4. Gwen Wallace, 'Report of Task Group on Local Management of Schools' (Mimeograph, p. 17). To be published in Gwen Wallace, ed., *Local Management of Schools: Research and Experience*, (forthcoming).
5. Formula funding was brought in by Circular 7/88. This stated that LMS was to have a four year introduction, from 1 April 1990 to 1 April 1994. However Circular 7/91 (April 1991) accelerated the time table, allowing all schools to control their budgets from 1 April 1992, instead of 1994. *Education*, 26 April 1991.
6. Ibid. See Circular 7/91.
7. Ibid.
8. Circular 7/88.
9. Gwen Wallace, op. cit., chapter by Tim Lee. See also Will Guy and Ian Mentor, 'Local Management of Resources: Who Benefits?' in Dawn Gill and Barbara Major (eds.), *Race and Education: Strategies for Change*, Open University Reader, forthcoming.
10. Wallace, op. cit., though this study includes contrary evidence by different authors. See also an important research study commissioned by the AMMA: R.J. Campbell and S.R. St J. Neill, *The Work Loads of Secondary School Teachers, An Interim Report*, University of Warwick, March 1991.
11. Alan Smithers and Pamela Robinson, *Staffing Secondary Schools in*

the Nineties, August 1991. This research concludes that 'the National Curriculum requires more teachers than heads can pay for under the Government's Local Management of Schools scheme'. *Independent*, 30 August 1991.

12. *Education*, 26 April 1991.
13. AMMA survey (see note 10).
14. Julian Haviland, *Take Care, Mr. Baker!*, London 1988, summarises many responses to this consultation paper, see pp. 167-189; see also Brian Simon, *Bending the Rules*, pp. 59-69.
15. See, for instance, A. Stillman and K. Maychell, *Choosing Schools: Parents, LEAs and the 1980 Education Act*, Windsor 1986.
16. Frank Echols, Andrew McPherson and J. Douglas Willms, 'Parental Choice in Scotland', mimeograph, Centre for Educational Sociology, University of Edinburgh, 1990.
17. Ibid., pp. 14-15.
18. Ibid., p. 18. The reference here is to Thatcher's personal intervention in 1988 to prevent the comprehensivisation of Paisley grammar school; see Echols *et al*, op. cit., p. 6.
19. *Education*, 12 July 1991.
20. *Times Educational Supplement*, 5 July 1991.
21. *Education*, 19 July 1991.
22. *Independent*, 18 July 1991; *Guardian*, 16 July 1991; this latter article claims that parental choice is, in fact, being dramatically *reduced* for many parents.
23. One of the first such analyses, the results of which were very striking, was made in the Central Advisory Council for Education (England) report entitled *Early Leaving* (1954); the CAC's next report, *15 to 18* (the Crowther report, 1959) also contained an extensive analysis of this phenomenon, as did the Robbins report *Higher Education* (1963).
24. Andrew McPherson, 'Social and Political Aspects of the Devolved Management of Scottish Secondary Schools', *Scottish Educational Review*, Vol.21, No.2, November 1989.
25. John Fitz and David Halpin, ' "From a sketchy policy, to a workable scheme": the DES and Grant Maintained Schools', mimeograph, 1991, pp. 22-3.
26. *Education*, 29 March 1991.
27. *Times Educational Supplement*, 11 January 1991.
28. Fitz and Halpin, op. cit., p. 29.
29. *Education*, 19 July 1991.
30. Local Schools Information (LSI), *Opting Out: the Case in 1991* (Broadsheet). In July 1991, 'Choice in Education', the government supported unit advocating opting out, released their own figures. They claimed an accelerating tendency – six times as many schools held ballots in the academic year 1990-91 compared to the previous year (183 compared to only 34 in 1989-90). Another 34 were due to vote before the end of the summer term. They claimed 96 schools as having successfully opted out; 105 had voted to opt out and were waiting approval by the DES; 18 had had their applications rejected; 61 had voted against opting out. *Education*, 12 July 1991.
31. *Times Educational Supplement*, 3 May 1991.
32. *Education*, 12 April 1991.

33. *Times Educational Supplement*, 12 April 1991.
34. *Education*, 3 May 1991.
35. *Times Educational Supplement*, 28 June 1991. Under immense pressure from local authorities, Clarke reduced the grant to opted-out schools from 16 to 15 per cent of their basic funding early in October. *Education*, 11 October 1991.
36. *Times Educational Supplement*, 19 July 1991.
37. Councillor Byers, Chair of the Association of Metropolitan Authorities, quoted in *Education*, 19 July 1991.
38. *Education*, 19 July 1991.
39. Ibid.
40. *Guardian*, 7 August 1991.
41. LSI, op. cit., (note 30).
42. *Education*, 3 May 1991. The Kingswood (Bristol) CTC is sponsored by the Wolfson Foundation and by Cable and Wireless PLC; that in Derby by Trusthouse Forte and the Landau Foundation.
43. Ibid.
44. *Times Educational Supplement*, 29 March 1991.
45. *Guardian*, 20 May 1991.
46. *Independent*, 3 April 1991; *Observer*, 21 April 1991.
47. *Times Educational Supplement*, 21 June 1991.
48. Ibid., 5 July 1991.
49. *Education*, 12 July 1991.
50. Ibid.
51. *Guardian*, 12 July 1991.
52. Ibid., 23 July 1991.
53. Ibid.
54. Geoffrey Walford and Henry Miller, *City Technology College*, Milton Keynes 1991, p. 169.
55. Asher Cashden and Des Wilson, 'Assessment: the state of the art', *Education*, 26 April 1991 (Digest).
56. *Times Educational Supplement*, 18 February 1991.
57. Ibid., 15 January 1991.
58. Ibid., 7 June 1991.
59. *Education*, 29 March 1991.
60. *Guardian*, 9 May 1991.
61. *Times Educational Supplement*, 16 June 1991.
62. *Times Educational Supplement*, 26 July 1991.
63. Ibid., 5 June 1991.
64. Demitri Coryton, *Education*, 5 July 1991.
65. *Education*, 5 June 1991.
66. Ibid., 5 July 1991.
67. On A levels and GCSE, Major said, 'If the transition from GCSE to A levels is causing difficulties, we must level GCSE up, not lower A level standards.' *Times Educational Supplement*, 12 July 1991. For the reactions of Examination Boards and others, Ibid.
68. *Education*, 5 July 1991.
69. *Times Educational Supplement*, 12 July 1991.
70. Ibid., 19 July 1991.
71. See the chronology of these clashes in ibid., 26 July 1991.
72. *Independent*, 19 July 1991. Griffiths is international adviser to the City firm of Goldman Sachs.

73. *Times Educational Supplement*, 26 July 1991.
74. Ibid., 12 July 1991.
75. Ibid.
76. *Independent*, 19 July 1991. The *Guardian* reported that 'Tories have been amazed that Philip Halsey ... seemed so impervious to first coded messages and then outright criticism of [SEAC's] actions,' 19 July 1991.
77. *Guardian*, 19 July 1991.
78. *Education*, 26 July 1991.
79. *Times Educational Supplement*, 26 July 1991.
80. *Education*, 19 July 1991.
81. *Independent*, 19 July 1991.
82. *Times Educational Supplement*, 26 July 1991.
83. Ibid., 9 August, 1991. The official reason for the replacement of Black and six other members of the NCC was that their 'terms of office' had expired. Replacements included two CTC governors and a former adviser on the Central Policy Review staff, *Education*, 9 August 1991.
84. Ibid., 26 July 1991.
85. *Education*, 26 July 1991.
86. *Times Educational Supplement*, 26 July 1991.
87. *Independent*, 31 July 1991.
88. *Times Educational Supplement*, 28 June 1991.
89. *Education*, 28 June 1991. In June the Society of Education Officers published a clear statement entitled 'Organisation of Local Government: the Future of the Education Service'. This announced the society's decision 'to play a major part in the debates that will take place in the coming months'.
90. *Times Educational Supplement*, 5 July 1991.
91. *Daily Telegraph*, 25 July 1991.
92. *Guardian*, 19 July 1991.
93. *Education*, 26 July 1991.
94. Ibid.
95. Ibid.
96. Lord Taylor, reported in *Education*, 21 June 1991 (from *Governors Action*, published by Action for Governors Information and Training).
97. *A New Partnership for Our Schools* (the Taylor Report), London 1977.
98. *Report of the Committee of Inquiry into the Education of Handicapped Children and Young People* (the Warnock Report), London 1978.
99. *Times Educational Supplement*, 9 August 1991; the quotations are from Warnock's article 'Equality Fifteen Years On', in the *Oxford Review of Education*, Vol.17, No.2.
100. *Guardian*, 23 July 1991.

Name Index

Subject Index

Adam Smith Institute, 100, 102, 132-3
Advisory Centre for Education, 157
advisory services (LEA), 68, 148, 189
age-weighting (LMS), 149-50
apprenticeship, 112, 128-9
Arnewood School, 163
assessment, 10, 28, 77-8, 81, 122, 134, 136-8, 145, 158-9, 174-9, 181-2, 183-4; *see also* testing
Assisted Places Scheme, 21, 43-4, 55, 86, 104
Association of County Councils, 191
Association of Metropolitan Authorities, 46, 165
attainment targets, 81
Audenshawe High School (Tameside), 68
Audit Commission, 51, 65-6, 152, 181, 188, 193

Bacup and Rawtenstall Grammar School, 68
Barnet, 61
Battersea Park School, 63
Bedfordshire, 66
Beechen Cliff School (Bath), 66-7
Black Papers, 126, 137-8, 139
Bourn Primary School (Lincs), 163
Bradford, 53
Bradford CTC, 59
Bridgnorth, 60
Brighton CTC, 59, 61, 169
British Association, 115-16
British Education and Management Society, 9
British Educational Research Association, 10, 72, 74, 87, 89
Bromley, 165
Bryce Commission, 95

Cambridge University, 95
Cambridgeshire, 19
Campaign for the Advancement of State Education, 31
Canada, 129
Castle Rushen School (Isle of Man), 53
central control (of education), 25, 133, 137, 145, 177, 196
central services (of LEAs), 68, 148-9, 166
Centre for Applied Research in Education, 72-5
Centre for Policy Studies, 170-1, 182-3, 185, 186
Chelsea, 24
choice, parental, 17, 56, 69, 135-6, 145, 152-3, 155, 156-9, 175
Choice in Education Ltd, 58, 68
churches, the, 31, 46, 64, 152, 165
Circular 10/65, 52-3
Circular 7/88, 146-7
Citizen's Charter, 180, 181-2, 183, 188-90, 193
city technology colleges, 7, 9, 21-2, 26, 32, 39, 41-2, 43, 49-50, 56-7, 59-64, 69, 84, 85-6, 90, 114, 134, 145, 168-74, 182, 192, 195, 197
City Technology Colleges Trust, 50, 57, 63, 171
Clarendon Commission, 95-6
Colleges of Further Education, 120
Colyton Grammar School (Devon), 68
competition (between schools), 8, 19-20, 22-3, 39-41, 42-3, 83, 85, 89, 91, 100, 102ff, 107-8, 114, 132, 144, 152
comprehensive education, 9, 18, 25, 34-5, 76-7, 82-3, 84, 87, 90-1, 99, 125, 130, 136-7, 138,